INTRODUCTION

Carroll County, Mississippi, was formed in 1833 from Indian lands as a result of the Choctaw Cession. All divorces and wills found from that time up to 1875 were abstracted. The original documents are available at the Carroll County Courthouse at Carrollton, Mississippi, and microfilm copies are available at the Mississippi State Archives.

Will Book A was searched page by page. The first will was recorded in August 1834. Several wills were found which were not listed in the will book index and others in the index were listed under incorrect names, causing them to be inaccessible to researchers. Names of slaves have been included where given in the will. Residences were all Carroll County, Mississippi, except where noted otherwise.

The only divorce records found in the Carroll County Courthouse for 1857 through 1875 were in three volumes of Chancery Court records. These volumes were unindexed and were searched page by page. No divorce records were found for the period before 1857.

^^*^*^*^*^*^*^*^*^*^*^*^*

Other Books By The Author

Marriages and Deaths from Mississippi Newspapers:
Volume 1 - 1837-1863

Published 1987 By

HERITAGE BOOKS, INC.
1540E Pointer Ridge Place, Bowie, Maryland, 20716
301-390-7708

ISBN 1-55613-082-1

TABLE OF CONTENTS

CHANCERY MINUTE BOOK I

FIRST DISTRICT, CARROLL COUNTY

April Term, 1857, p9

MARGARET C. R. GRISWOOD
-vs-
SYLVESTER W. GRISWOOD

On the 21st day of April, 1857, before Judge Joel M. Acker, Margaret C. R. Griswood charged her husband with more than three years desertion of herself and three small children. The marriage was dissolved and the complainant restored to the rights of feme sole. The defendant was to pay costs of the proceeding.

October Term, 1857, p20

HENRY HUFFMAN -vs- MINERVA HUFFMAN

Henry Huffman charged his wife Minerva with willfully and without any cause abandoning him for three years and also for adultrous intercourse with D. K. Aiken. The Bonds of Matrimony were dissolved and complainant was to pay costs of the suit. Signed, sealed and ordered October 28th, 1857, by Judge W. Cothran.

October Term, 1857, p26

ROBERT I. McGREELY -vs- HARRIETT A. McGREELY

Robert McGreely charged his wife Harriett A. with willful, continued and obstinate desertion of him for three years. The Bonds of Matrimony were dissolved and complainant was to pay costs. Signed, sealed and ordered the 31st day of October, 1857, by Judge W. Cothran.

October Term, 1858, p70

EMILY J. WIGGINS -vs- A. J. WIGGINS

Complainant is allowed to file an amended Bill and the defendant Alexander is to pay her Eight dollars per month as her alimony, and to pay in quarterly installments. Signed Oct. 28, 1858, by Judge W. Cothran.

October Term, 1858, p70

W. H. H. PHIPPS -vs- R. JANE PHIPPS

The parties were married in the State of Mississippi. The complainant charged the defendant with willful abandonment for the space of three years. The Bonds of Matrimony were dissolved and the parties were at liberty to remarry. The complainant was to pay costs. Signed by Judge W. Cothran.

30 October 1858, p73

THOMAS J. FULLILOVE
-vs-
MARY FULLILOVE (nee Geren)

The court was satisfied that there were good grounds for divorce and did decree that the marriage which was solomized on the 8th of July, 1858, be disolved and annulled. The complainant was to pay the cost of this suit. Ordered by Judge W. Cothran.

No date, p81

EMILY J. WIGGINS -vs- ALEXANDER WIGGINS

The court decreed that the property mentioned in the bill of complaint is the property of the complainant and that she is entitled to the notes mentioned and to the hire of her slaves. The defendant had been guilty of adultry and a divorce is granted to the complainant and she is free to remarry. It is also ordered that the defendant, Alexander Wiggins, shall not be at liberty to marry again and he shall remain in law a married person. Defendant was to pay court costs. Signed 23rd day of April, 1859, by Judge W. Cothran.

20 April 1860, p117

FRANCIS SUGGS -vs- ROBERT SUGGS

Defendant Robert Suggs is a non-resident of the State of Mississippi. He was accused of having adultrous intercourse with a woman named in depositions. Divorce was granted and Francis Suggs is freed from all obligations to Robert Suggs, but Robert Suggs being the offending party shall not be at liberty to remarry, and shall remain at law a married person. Signed by Judge W. Cothran.

No date, p162

W. D. TROTTER -vs- SARAH TROTTER

The defendant is a non-resident of this State. The Bonds of Matrimony were dissolved and W. D. Trotter given custody of the child. The complainant was to pay costs of proceedings. Signed 18 April 1861 by Judge W. Cothran.

No date, p184

J. ANNIE BASKIN -vs- R. P. BASKIN

The Bonds of Matrimony were dissolved and complainant restored to rights of feme sole. The complainant was to pay costs. 9 September 1862; Signed by Judge W. Cothran.

13 April 1864, p189

CHARLES SLAVENS -vs- JULIA SLAVENS

The defendant had been guilty of adultry and the Bonds of Matrimony were dissolved. The complainant was to pay costs of proceedings. Signed by Judge W. Cothran.

13 April 1864, p189

MARGARET I. HOOD -vs- SAMUEL I. HOOD

Motion for alimony. The complainant and her child were in destitution and the defendant was ordered to pay to Richard Small, as trustee for the comfort of the complainant, $300 per annum, commencing from the 1st day of January, 1864, to be paid in quarterly payments. Signed by Judge W. Cothran.

14 April 1864, p190

ELIZABETH CAIN -vs- WM. I. CAIN

The defendant had been guilty of adultry with the negro woman Mary. The Bonds of Matrimony were annulled, dissolved and set aside, and the defendant was to pay costs. Signed by Judge W. Cothran.

21 October 1864, p193

E. J. N. McKAY -vs- N. A. E. McKAY

The defendant committed adultry and therefore the Bonds of Matrimony between the complainant and defendant were dissolved. The complainant was given custody and control of the children begotten by him and defendant. The complainant was ordered to pay defendant the amount of twelve hundred dollars in treasury notes of the Confederate States of America, generally known as Confederate money. Complainant is to pay costs of the suit. Signed by W. Cothran, Judge.

20 April 1866, p201-202

MARY A. TATE -vs- THOMAS L. TATE

Thomas Tate has been guilty in the year 1860 of adultry with a certain woman named Menerva and in the year 1865, adultry with another woman named Henrietta, in the county of Sunflower in this State. Bonds of Matrimony were dissolved and annulled. Defendant to pay cost of suit. W. Cothran, Judge.

April Term, 1866, p206

MARY J. HOOD -vs- SAMUEL J. HOOD

Ordered citation issued to defendant to show cause that he not be charged with contempt of court in failing to pay to complainant the alimony due her.

27 October 1866, p219

NORMAN M. YEWELL -vs- JANE YEWELL

Bonds of Matrimony dissolved and Norman M. Yewell is relieved from any legal restraint or disability to contract matrimony hereafter. Complainant to pay costs of proceedings. W. Cothran, Judge.

19 April 1867, p240-241

LAURA BARHAM -vs- JAMES N. BARHAM

Bonds of Matrimony dissolved, complainant to pay costs. W. Cothran, Judge.

17 October 1869, p267

JEFFERSON MAY -vs- AMANDA MAY

Bonds of Matrimony were dissolved, complainant to pay costs. W. Cothran, Judge.

25 October 1869, p276

MARGARET J. HOOD -vs- SAMUEL J. HOOD

Margaret J. Hood charged with deserting the bed and board of Sara Samuel J. Hood for more than four years. It was ordered that she cease and be satisfied on the payment of $100 council fees and the further sum of $100 to Margaret J. Hood, and no other sum. Sara Samuel J. Hood and Margaret Hood shall be divorced from the Bonds of Matrimony. Samuel Hood to pay costs of the suit.

19 October 1870, p461

PAULINE V. ESTIS -vs- WILLIAM J. ESTIS

Wm. J. Estis is a resident of Memphis, Tennessee. Pauline V. Estis was granted a divorce from the Bonds of Matrimony. She was also granted custody of her little boy. D. P. Coffy, Chancellor.

22 October 1870, p462

JOHN J. ROGERS -vs- REBECCA ROGERS

The defendant was found guilty of the acts of adultry as

charged, therefore the Bonds of Matrimony were dissolved. John J. Rogers to pay costs of suit. D. P. Coffey, Chancellor.

21 April 1871, p517

EMELINE MEIRS -vs- CARROLL MEIRS

Defendant had abandoned his wife, the complainant, since the summer of 1863. Bonds of Matrimony were dissolved and complainant declared feme sole and free to remarry. Child to be in custody of Emeline and defendant prohibited from interfering in any way with said child. Complainant to pay costs of suit. D. P. Coffey, Chancellor.

22 April 1871, p522

BEN KIMBELL -vs- MARY KIMBELL

The defendant was served with notice of suit and he failed to appear. The Bonds of Matrimony were dissolved and complainant was to pay costs of suit. D. P. Coffey, Chancellor.

24 April 1871, p523

BURT BURFORD -vs- MELISSA BURFORD

Burt & Melissa Burford were absolutely and forever divorced from the Bonds of Matrimony. It was ordered that Burt Burford, complainant, pay all costs. D. P. Coffey, Chancellor.

24 April 1871, p524

JESSEE HERRING -vs- CATHARINE HERRING

The court was satisfied that Catharine Herring committed the adultrous act with which she was charged and therefore the Bonds of Matrimony were dissolved, complainant paying costs of the suit. D. P. Coffey, Chancellor.

19 October 1871, p577

JIM HENRY -vs- JENNY LENA HENRY

Bonds of Matrimony were dissolved and no obstruction as to marrying again were placed on either party. D. P. Coffey, Chancellor.

23 October 1871, p583

GUS PURNELL -vs- SOPHIA PURNELL

The Bonds of Matrimony were dissolved and both parties were allowed to remarry and they were allowed to act as though he or she had never been married. D. P, Coffey, Chancellor.

25 October 1871, p591

ALECK BROWN -vs- SILVIA BROWN, alias **KELLY**

She was charged with unlawful cohabitation and acts of adultry in violation of sacred rights of matrimony. Bonds of Matrimony were forever dissolved. Complainant to pay costs of suit. D. P. Coffey, Chancellor.

6 April 1872, p649

LYDIA EDWARDS -vs- DANIEL O. EDWARDS

Bonds of Matrimony were dissolved and Lydia was authorized to contract marriage with any party she may see proper. D. P. Cofffey.

CHANCERY COURT FINAL RECORDS

VOLUME 4

October Term, 1872, p75

NED BINGHAM -vs- MARIA BINGHAM

Ned and Maria Bingham were both citizens of Carroll County when they married in July 1869. She was previously Maria McMillan. He charged that after living together two weeks she deserted him and continued this desertion for three years. And during that time that she had given birth to two children which were not his; therefore, he is charging her with adultry.

October Term, 1872, p76

DIMENT MOORE -vs- MARTHA MOORE

They were married and lived together until September 1870, when she deserted him.

October Term, 1872, p86

FELICITY S. STARKE -vs- THOS. H. STARKE

She stated that they were married in Carroll County in 1866 and resided there until 1871 when they went to the Choctaw Nation, Arkansas. She also stated that in November 1871 Thomas H. Starke abandoned her and their infant child and had not lived with her since. His whereabouts were unknown. She stated that she had two children from this marriage--one about two years old, the other born in February 1872. She owned separate property received from her late father, Samuel Long, which was in Carroll Co. Filed 16 Sept. 1872.

October Term, 1872, p167

MINERVA KENT -vs- SANDY KENT

Minerva Kent was a resident of Carroll County. Sandy Kent's location was unknown. They married and lived together about four months when he abandoned her, which was more than two years earlier. Filed 1 Nov. 1872.

October Term, 1872, p172

ANN ROCKFORD -vs- RICHARD ROCKFORD

They were marriad August 1867. She charged him with habitual, cruel and inhuman treatment, marked by personal violence toward her and desertion for more than two years. She also stated that he had brought disgrace upon himself by violation of the criminal laws for which indictments were presently pending against him. He was at the time a fugitive from justice. Filed 29 August 1872.

October Term, 1872, p233

CHARLES GREEN -vs- AMY GREEN

Charles Green was born in the State of Virginia and came to this state about 20 years prior to this. He married Amy M. L---- in August 1867 and they lived together until December 1868, when she deserted him. Filed 30 May 1873.

October Term, 1872, p290

LEWIS BRADSHAW -vs- MARGARET ANN BRADSHAW

Lewis Bradshaw was a citizen of Carroll County, Margaret a citizen of Leflore County. They married and lived together two years when she deserted him. Filed 17 Dec. 1873.

October Term, 1872, p471

GEORGE COOLEY -vs- ELIZA COOLEY

They were married in late 1869 or early 1870 in Jasper County, Mississippi, and they lived together in Jasper County until 1870, when she deserted him. Filed 29 Nov. 1873.

October Term, 1872, p479

LARKIN HEMPHILL -vs- HANNAH HEMPHILL

Larkin Hemphill married Hannah Cunningham in 1874* and they lived together as man and wife until the spring of 1866, when she abandoned him until the year 1869, at which time she removed to the State of Tennessee, where she had resided since. He also stated that she had been guilty of adultry. Filed 12 March 1874.

*Though it is obviously incorrect, this is the date noted in the record.

October Term, 1872, p481

DANIEL S. McDOUGALD -vs- RUTH H. P. McDOUGALD

They were married and lived together about two years and in March 1873 he and the defendant separated and ever since lived apart. He accused her of adultry. Filed 12 September 1874.

CHANCERY COURT FINAL RECORDS

VOLUME 5

April Term, 1875, p25

LOU MONEY -vs- HENRY MONEY

She charged that Henry deserted her and was presently a citizen of Leflore County. Their children were Isaac, John and Sally, the youngest about three and the oldest about eight years of age. She charged that he refused and neglected to contribute to the support of their children. She also accused him of taking up with a woman named Eliza Mallory (who is since dead). She asked for a divorce and custody of the children and financial support. Filed 12 March 1875.

April Term, 1875, p28

WESLEY TOWNSEND -vs- SOFFA TOWNSEND

Soffa Townsend was a citizen of Montgomery County. He charged that they lived together at her father's house about two months when she deserted him by not moving into a house he furnished for her. He believed she committed adultry as she had two children, whose father was unknown, during the abandonment. Filed 7 Dec. 1874.

April Term, 1875, p30

FRANK BURNBY -vs- LUCY BURNBY

Bill for Divorce - They were married in 1869 and they lived together about 18 months when she abandoned him. Filed 17 September 1875.

April Term, 1875, p75

HARRISON YOUNG -vs- WINNEY YOUNG

Both were residents of Carroll County. They were married on or about 13 January 1872. Her maiden name was Winney Gayden. He stated that he married unaware that his wife was totally deficient in the female genital organs and that after years of doctors bills hoping to correct the defect and being told that she was unable to become a wife to any man, he requested that his marriage contract be voided or a divorce granted. Filed 24 November 1875.

April Term, 1875, p92

LUCY WASHINGTON -vs- SAMPSON WASHINGTON

They were married in 1865 and they lived together until 1 Feb. 1875. During the latter part of this time he became very cruel to her, beating her. She also charged that since their separation he has been guilty of adultry with one Matilda Watson. There was only one child of this marriage, a girl about six years of age, and he has not provided for her. Filed 17 October 1876.

WILL BOOK A

WILLIAM JOHNSTON

Wife - Martha Johnston. At death of Martha Johnston negro woman Winny to be set free and estate to be divided between William Young, and William W. Dykes. Sister - Esther Lackey (her daughter Adaline Lackey mentioned). Executors - John W. Dykes, Hugh R. Young, Thomas Bovard, John I. McCoughan. Witnesses - Samuel B. Eskridge, Taliaferro Eskridge. 12 August 1834, p1.

THOMAS I. WHITE

Of Holmes Co., MS. Brother - Wm. D. White. Mother - Pamelia Stores. A bequeath to James Bunch. Executors - Mr. Persons of Carroll Co. and Dr. Crowder of Carroll Co. Witnesses - T. M. Scurlock, Wm. Hewes, J. S. Robertson, Richard Plugg, Jn. Edwards, Peter F. Gray. Slaves - Wilson, Lewis, Loney. 28 December 1834, p2.

JOSIAH ASHLEY

Wife - Nancey Ashley. Son - John Hardy Ashley. Executor - friend Jeptha K. Wooten. Witnesses - Jas. Wellons, H. F. Wooten, Daniel Wooten. Slave - Sophia. 6 February 1836, p3.

FRANCES BEASLEY.

Daughters - Sarah Green, Catharine Taylor. Granddaughter - Francis Taylor. Niece - Eliza Williams. Grandson - Robert Green. Executor - David O. Shattuck. Witnesses - Stephen Thompson, Jonathan Ray, Jacob Miller. Slaves - Mary, Dick, Hannah, Sophia, Lucinda, Maria, Lewis, Caroline, Jinny, Jim. 5 August 1836, p4.

DOUGLAS MERIWEATHER

Wife - Judith Meriweather. Children - Robert Emmett, John Nicholas, Thos. Paine, Charles James Fox, Mary Eliza Carrington. Executors - wife Judith and sons Robert Emmet Meriweather and John Nicholas Meriweather when they arrive at age 21. Witnesses - Elbridge G. Stevens, James M. Manomy, Jno. L. Irwin. 12 August 1837, p6.

GEORGE W. GREEN

Wife - Sarah Ann C. Green. Daughter - Martha Ann F. Green. Children of my brother - Archibald H. Green and Albert J. Green. Executors - wife Sarah Ann Green and David O. Shattuck. Witnesses - John J. Clow, Jonathan Ray, D. O. Shattuck. Slaves - Sillah; Celia & her 3 children Monroe, Miranda, & Anthony; Lewis; Noah; Mahula; Andre; Mary. 16 September 1837, p7.

MOSES LOCKARD

Wife - Elizabeth Lockard. Adopted child - Martha Caroline Curtis. Brothers - Alfred Lockard residing in the state of Tennessee, John Lockard, William Lockard, and Thomas Lockard. Sister - Keziah Lockard. Witnesses - Wm. B. Wallace and W. M. Stansbury. Slaves - Frank, Edie, Linsey, Anna Jane, Jerry. 13 June 1837, p8.

FLAVELL M. PORTER

Wife - Eliza R. Porter, gives property in State of New York. Daughter - Josephine Porter. Brothers - Samuel A. Porter and Timothy Porter. Property in Connecticut to be sold. Bequeath to children of John Flavel Bliss, dec'd. John F. Bliss & Homes Bliss (children of my sister Mary Ann Bliss). Executor - Samuel A. Porter. Witnesses - T. S. Ayres and T. Best. 30 November 1837, p9.

THOMAS L. ESKRIDGE

Wife - Julia A. Eskridge. Son - Rich. E. Eskridge. Other children mentioned but not named. Executors - Julia A. Eskridge and friend George Bamburg. Witnesses - Jno. Butt and Jno. A. Binford. 11 December 1837, p10.

ISAIAH BROWN

Wife - Mary Brown. Mentions children, no names. Executor - wife Mary Brown. Witnesses - Hutor McNeill, Elijah Sullivan, Caswell Redding. 4 August 1837. Probated April 1838, p11.

OLIVER CROSS

(Late of State of Virginia.) Wife - Ann Cross. Son - Fleming Cross. Mentions nine children, unnamed. Executors - Ann Cross, O. Fleming Cross, Jno. E. Palmer, Robert T. Cross. 31 May 1837. Probated September 1838, p12.

ROBERT PITMAN

(Formerly of State of North Carolina, Roberson County; now of St. Clair, State of Alabama.) Daughters - Celia Townsend, Susanna Moore, dec'd., wife of James Moore, Mary Thompson, Senith. Son - Caswell D. Pitman. Wife - Lucy/Lucresa Pittman. Executor - Caswell D. Pitman. Witnesses - C. C. P. Farrar, Jno. F. Dill, Arthur G. Green
Slaves - Nancy, Alfred, Caira, Little Lewis, Chany, Baccus, Jude, Lewis, Bet, Venus, Bess, Stephen. 30 March 1838, p13.

HANNAH WOOD

(Of Franklin County, Tennessee.) Nephews - Andrew Woods, son of James Woods of Franklin County, Tennessee; James Woods. Nieces - Hannah Ruth Woods, dau. of aforesaid James Woods, and Hannah Woods, daughter of Andrew Woods. Executors - James Woods and Wm. Woods. Witnesses - Richard C. Arnett, Abigail Woods. Slaves - Samuel, Talbot, Albert, America. 25 March 1833, p14.

SAMUEL MARSH

Son - Samuel B. Marsh. Grandson - Sam. B. Jones. Granddaughters - Elizabeth A. Jones & Martha Buckhold. Stepsons - Allen B. Addison & James Y. Blocker. Stepdaughter - Adaline Goddart. Executor - Samuel B. Marsh. Witnesses - James Minter, Geo. A. Addison. Slaves - Margaret, Dow, Creary. 17 April 1838. Probated October 1839, p15.

URIAH NEWMAN

Brothers - Josiah Newman and Reuben B. Newman.Mother - Elizabeth Newman. Nieces - Frances Irwin, Elizabeth Newman. Executors - Reuben B. Newman, Josiah Newman & Reuben Gaydon. Witnesses - Reuben B. Newman, Bartlet N. Eddes, Nathan Simpson, D. C. McLeod, and John McCaskill. Slaves - Abram, Ama, America, Alexander, Sam, Goloway, Fanny, Anna, Caroline, Jane, George, Dick, Isabell, Yellow Mary, Susan, Tom, James, Marsha, Elmira, John, Harrott, Nancy, Eliza, Nelson, Almedia, William, Mary. 6 September 1839. Probated October 1839, p15.

THOMAS TYLER

Sons - Elisha, Philip, Lenir, Dorrell, Washington, Thomas. Sons-in-law - Warren Jennings, Daniel Holman. Daughters - Mary Tyler, Elizabeth Tyler. Wife mentioned but not named. Executors - Elisha Tyler and Philip Tyler. Witnesses - Jno. A. Binford, Jno. P. Taylor, William Grant. Slaves - Caroline,

Lucy, Margaret, January, Lydia, Jane, Ellick, Charlotte, Rachel, Andrew, Phorh, Moses. 1 January 1840. Probated May 1841, p17.

HENRY SANDERS

Wife - Jane Sanders. Grandson - Newton Corbin. Mentioned - William B. Corbin. Legatee - Presley Sanders Ezell. Executor - Moses B. Harrell. Witnesses - A. Harrell, John W. Harrell. Slave - Judah. 18 August 1840. Probated October 1841, p18.

LEVI L. MORRIS

(Nuncupative will.) Probate Court - November 1841, p19. Statement - Levi L. Morris died about the middle of June 1840, appointed Richard Morris and Robert Clark executors. Testified to by William N. Miller and Briggs Barker. Wife and children mentioned but not named.

ANDREW GRAHAM

(Nuncupative will.) Probate Court - January 1841. Statement - Andrew Graham died latter part of 1840, bequeathed all property to Douglass Robinson, son of Alfred B. Robinson. Testified to by Reuben B. Newman and Alfred B. Robinson. Probated January 1841, p19.

THOMAS JEFFERSON HAWKINS

(Nuncupative will.) Father - Caleb Hawkins. Sisters - Mary A. McClellane, Ann W. Gee, Catherine Withers. Niece - Mary F. Hawkins. Brother - Thomas Hawkins. Slave - David. Signed by Thos. Hawkins and Mary A. McClellane, 1 March 1841. 29 September 1840, p20.

JAMES KING

Wife - Lucy King. Sons - Daniel King and John King. Daughter - Nancy Raspberry. Other children - Polly Norman, Lucy Ann Davis, George W., Sarah McCalister and Elizabeth. Granddaughter - Elmira J. Davis. Witnesses - Wm. Thompson and C. G. Parsons. Slaves - Briant, Rose, Jordan, Lewis. 2 March 1841. Probated - May 1841, p20.

WINFRED SPICER

(Of Yalobusha County, Mississippi.) Grandson - Robert M. Spicer. Children of Robert M. Spicer - John E., Eliza C., Robert A., Samuel S., Nancy C. and James C. Spicer. Executor - Robert M. Spicer. Witnesses - Samuel M. Hankins, Wm. M. Hankins, Jno. E. Baker. Slaves - Grace, Delpha,

George, Peter, John, Minerva, Maria, Lewis, Washington, Jackson, Matilda, Fanny, Henry, Jem, Dolly. 19 July 1839. Probated - June 1841, p21.

LOUISA R. B. PEYTON

Sisters - Lucy, wife of James W. Eskridge; and Mary Peyton Money is due Louisa R. B. Peyton from State of Virginia. Witnesses - W. Brooks, Wm. C. Eskridge, and J. L. L. Brooke. 1 December 1840. Probated - July 1841, p23.

ALLEN SHARKEY

Children - Sarah Pate, Greenwood L. Sharkey, Allen N. Sharkey. Friends - William Terry, Duncan C. McLeod, W. W. Burkhead. Executors - son-in-law Joel H. Pate, Robert R. Sharkey, and Patrick Sharkey. Witnesses - Jno. M. Maury, W. Terry, D. C. McLeod. Slave - Miley. 7 September 1841. Probated - October 1841, p24.

JOSHUA COLLINS

Wife _ Sarah Collins. Sons - Wilson Collins, John Collins and James Collins. Daughters-in-law - Milly Collins, wife of son Jacob Collins and Harriett C. Collins, wife of son James Collins. Executors - Sarah Collins and James Collins. Witnesses - Titus Howard, Henry T. Howard, Lewis T. Howard. Slaves - Ishume and his wife Harriett, Jacks, Bidy, Abraham, Rose, Anthony, Mary. 23 April 1840. Probated - December 1840, p26.

ANN ROSS

Sons - William B. Ross and James D. Ross, deceased. Daughters - Ann Ross and Charity Ann Johnson, wife of Allen A. Johnson. Four Grandsons, unnamed. Two Granddaughters, unnamed. Executor - Wm. B. Ross. Witnesses - R. Gaydon and Allen A. Johnson. 24 November 1840. Probated - February 1842, p27.

JAMES B. CROWDER

Mother - Lucy Crowder. Witness - Wm. R. Hodges. Slaves - Henry and his wife Eliza, Isaac. 28 August 1838. Probated - March 1842, p27.

JAMES MCMANOMY

Wife - Katharine McManomy. Children - Marion, Miriam, Amanda, James Lafayette, Baron DeCalb. Executors - friends James Collins and Treadwell S. Ayres. Witnesses -

William Shinpock, Jacob Collins, Jesse Howard. Slave - Maw. Probated - June 1842, p29.

HOWARD B. HOWSE

Sisters - Katharine O. Howse of Onslow, North Carolina and Nancy C. Duffy, wife of Charles Duffy both of Onslow, North Carolina. Brother - James T. Howse, given interest in land in the Republic of Texas. Executor - James T. Howse. Witnesses - Wilson Collins, George R. Carroll, Richmond Carroll. 19 July 1842. Probated - October 1842, p30.

WILLIAM COUCH

Wife - Elenor Couch. Children - Emily Couch, John Couch, and Mary Couch. Witnesses - Zachariah Blackman, Wm. N. Sprawls, Wm. Ferguson. 2 August 1842. Probated - November 1842, p31. (Note: Elenor Couch remarried Elijah Langford, Carroll County, Mississippi, 29 June 1844.)

JANE ESTILL

Sons - James, Henderson and Samuel. Daughters - Sally Yates, wife of Wm. Yates (now living in Kentucky), Mary Ann Day, Susan Bealer, Ruth McWhorter, Jane Doyle, wife of Wm. G. Doyle. Mentioned - Cyrus McWhorter. Executors - Martin Nelms and Andrew Woods. Witnesses - W. G. Herring, W. Wilson, John McLean. Slaves - Nelson, Sicily, Orlena, Amelia, Minerva, Anderson, Katy, John and his wife Young Cicily, Fred, Rhodes, Freeman (Grace his wife and two children Henry and Catharine), Frederick to have his freedom. 24 March 1841, p31.

WILLIAM CLARK

(Of Abbeville, South Carolina). Nephew - William Clark. Bequeath to oldest daughter of deceased brother Patrick C. Clark. Witnesses - James C. Calhoun, James W. Harris, Bartty Tucker. Slaves - Alick, Tom, Sidney, John, Jane, Pelinas, Charles, Mary, Henry, Patrick, Sarah, Julia, Alfred, Cesar. 1 November 1841, p33.

JOHN P. TAYLOR

Two youngest sons - Benjamin B. Taylor and Nathaniel Taylor. Mentions wife and other children, unnamed. Executor - Benjamin B. Taylor. Witnesses - John W. Dikes, Hugh Rodgers, Wiley Carr, Francis Lewis. 9 February 1843, p34.

JOSEPH PERSON

Wife - Sarah Person. Sons - Peterson, Henry, Turner, Presly,

John. Daughters - Sarah, Emily, Elizabeth, Martha, Nancy. Mentions land in Fayette County, Tennessee. Executors - Sarah Person and Peterson Person. Witnesses - Thomas Jefferson, David W. Jefferson, George W. Roach, Henry A. Roach. Slaves - Hilliary, Philip, Jesse, Direna, Mary, Anderson, Albert, Let, Teen, Eliza, Harriet, Willis. 2 September 1837, p35.

MARTIN NELMS

Father - David Nelms. Mother - Unity Nelms of Franklin County, Georgia. Executors - William Y. Colein, Henry M. Merritt. Witnesses: - D. M. Lipscomb, James O. Doyle. 1 May 1843, p36.

WILLIAM SHAMBURGER

Wife - Susan Shamburger. Daughters - Rebecca Jane Shamburger and Ureatha Shamburger. Sons - William Franklin, Madison Wilson, Ulysses Lafayette. Father - Peter Shamburger, dec'd. of North Carolina. Executor - John H. Wilson and William Bennett. Witnesses - Thomas Pleasant, John Ferguson, Milton A. Wilson. Slaves - Joshua, Pelina, Hannah, Clarey, Ralph, Salestine, Bill, Roseann, Nelson, Jerry, Tom. 28 March 1843, p37. (Note: Susan Shamburger married Hugh Barfield, Carroll County, Mississippi, 21 April 1846.)

ELINER MAXWELL

(Of Duplin County, North Carolina). Daughters - Margaret Pearsall, Sarah Stanford, Dorothy Ann Moon, Cassandra Moon. Son - Dickson Slone. Granddaughters - Clarissa McGowan and Ann Eliza Slone. Grandson - David Moore. Brother - James Dickson. Executor - James Dickson. Witness - Susana Dickson. Slaves - Luke, Mary, Pheribe, Rachel, Kitty, Laura, Bill, Colt, Goodson, Harry, Eliza. 31 October 1832, p38.

LEWIS MILLER

Wife - Sybil Miller. Children - Martha, Sybil, Lavenia, Elizabeth, Catharine, Ann Francis, Joseph Benson, Philip McKindre, John William. Executor - Friend & relative, John B. Koonce. Witnesses - G. A. Graves and L. C. Maclin. 4 August 1843. Probated - October 1843, p40.

JAMES D. McLEAN

Daughters - Nancy L. Levan, Eliza D. Hanna, Mary Martha Neill. Sons - John S., Georga D., James M., Ephraim R. Executors - Four sons listed above. Witnesses - A. Newton,

Sam'l H. Young, James A. Parmele. Slaves - Mary, Amanda, Riley, Henry, Parish, Calaway, Rachel, Jerucia, Mariah, Caroline, Naks, Ellick, Laura, Lewis to be emancipated. 5 January 1843, p40.

JAMES KELLY

Daughters - Jane Goodson, Eliza Cottingham. Sons - Wiley Kelly, Robert Kelly. Granddaughter - Jane Hall. Executors - Wiley and Robert Kelly. Witnesses - C. M. Vaiden, H. H. Weir. Slaves - Stephen; Maria; Elizabeth; Boy Thomas and his wife Hannah and her five children Caroline, Elizabeth, Dolly, Martha, and Thomas; Sarah. 30 March 1844, p43.

JOHN M. ELLIS

Youngest brother - William Ellis, resident of Orange County, North Carolina. Executors - Wm. W. Whitehead, Hugh W. Davis, Thomas A. Watkins. Witnesses - Wm. Hemingway, Obadiah Echols, Lewis H. Davis. 8 May 1844, p43.

THOMAS DENT

Wife - Mag Dent. Brother - Wallin C. Dent (father of Malcolm Dent). Bequeaths to heirs of Harriet Beall, heirs of Walter Dent, Chloe S. Beall, Amelia S. Johnson, Nancy T. Beall, Louisa Hasty, Phella B. Hughes & Otho B. Dent. Executors - Russell G. Beall and Otho B. Dent. Witness - Francis Harrell. 23 April 1836. Probated - August 1844, p44.

HARDY WOOTAN

Wife - Judy Wootan. Children - Calvit, Artymissa and Masey. Witnesses - Jno. J. Hodge, W. N. Miller, Joseph Drake. Slave - Sally. 26 September 1840, p44. (Note: Newspaper *Mississippi Democrat*, Carrollton, Mississippi, dated 9 September 1846 lists heirs of Hardy Wooten as Judath, Artimissa, Calvet, Moses, and Elizabeth.)

JAMES T. HOWSE

Wife - Susannah A. Howse. Daughter - Olive H. Howse. Sisters - Catharine O. Foy and Nancy C. Duffy, both of North Carolian. Brother - Howard B. Howse. Executors - Titus Howard and Orman S. Kimbrough. Witnesses - Samuel Moore, Lewis T. Howard, O. L. Kimbrough. Slave - Charity. 6 August 1844, p45.

LOUISA E. GERALD

Daughters - Erin A., wife of Alfred R. Drake and Vidan M., wife of Algenon S. S. Newton. Executors - Richard W. Graves and Algernon S. S. Newton. Witnesses - B. Phinney, Geo. A. Hogsett, G. W. H. Marr. Slaves - Lucy, Bill, Sally, Cerilla, Jacob. 15 January 1843, p46.

CHARLES G. SPANN

(Of Noxubee County, Mississippi.) Wife - Ann C. Spann. Children mentioned but not named. Executor - wife. Witnesses - Philix Clayton, Ansal G. Cunningham, George H. Cathcort. Slave - Britton. 6 June 1840, p47.

CHARLES CAWTHON

Sons - John C., Clarburn, Charles M. Wilkerson T., James T. Daughters - Tabitha Nelm, Francis Kemp, Elizabeth Bartlett. Executor - Lewis Wimberly. Witnesses - Lewis Kimberly, James A. Lundy, Jos. R. Young. Slaves - Harriet Malinda and her three children Josiah (age 5), Jeremiah (age 3), Harriet (age 1) to be freed; Eliza and her child John (2 months old); Clark. 24 April 1845, p48.

MARY LUCAS

(Of Chatham County, North Carolina.) Deceased Husband - George Lucas. Daughters - Mary Taylor, Sarah Ann Geren. Granddaughter - Apphia Taylor. Grandsons - James Taylor, Philip Taylor, William Taylor. Executors - Grandson George W. Taylor and Green Womack. Witnesses - J. C. Williams, Jno. J. Goodwin. Slaves - Jesse, Affy, Joh, Sampson, Robert, Charles. 3 January 1832, p50.

ELIJAH M. RUSSELL

Wife - Susan Russell. Sisters - Rebecca Russell, Nancy Russell & Elizabeth Russell. Executors - Stephen Terry and Joseph Drake. Witnesses - B. S. Rhea and Jno. S. Goodall. No date, p52.

FENELER ARNOLD

Notes on Alexander Gray to be collected. Daughter - Polly Howard. Sons - George Gray, Alexander Gray and James W. Gray. Executors - James W. Gray and Titus Howard. Witnesses - James Blank, Lewis T. Howard, H. M. Stinson. 12 March 1834, p52.

BENJ. SYKES, Sr.

(Of Tuscaloosa County, Alabama.) Son - Benj. Sykes, Jr. Daughter - Sarah Sykes. Wife and another daughter mentioned but not named. Witnesses - H. W. Colin, Thos. Travis, J. I. Ormand. 27 September 1845, p53.

JOHN PURNELL

(Of Halifax County, North Crolina.) Sons - William D., Robert, Thomas, Mingo T., Micajah T., Henry M. Daughters - Mary Purnell and Rebecca Sledge. Sister - Susan Wharton, widow of Julius Wharton, dec'd. Mentioned purchase of lands from Landon Clanton, Robert L. Marshall, Alexes Marshall, Frances Legrand, and Dick Byrd; Lemuel Long, Rice B. Pierce. Executors - sons John, Henry, and William. Witnesses - Rice B. Pierce and Margaret B. Pierce. Slaves - Davy; Sam; Archer; Big Lewis; Ben; Little Liz; Tom; Till; Beck and her children Sterling, Matt, Davy, Fanny, and Henry; Prescilla; Bynum; Delier; Charles; Frank; Little Will; Ola; Sarah. Year only available - 1835, p56.

ELIZABETH E. KING

Daughter - Elizabeth M. King. Father - Merritt Dillard. Brothers - Josiah M. Dillard, Joseph Dillard. Sister - Mary E. Carpenter. Executor - Merritt Dillard. Witnesses - A. W. King and I. T. Lane. Slave - Clarcy. 4 May 1846, p57.

DAVID COFFIULA

Wife - Elizabeth Coffiula. Sisters - Sarah Gilbert, Ruth Calhoun, wife of Ross Calhoun. Bequeaths to Lucy Ann Cain, wife of William T. Cain; Riley Stoop; William Stoop; Alexander and Catharine Harper. Executors - Benjamin F. Harper and William T. Cain. Witnesses - Sam'l. Hairston, Daniel McEachern, Sam'l. Hart. Slaves - Willis and his wife Elizabeth and their daughter Juliann; Henry; Caroline; Allen. 29 May 1846, p58.

ELIZABETH COFFIELD

Renunciation. She renounced all claim to any bequest of her husband's will. Husband - David Coffield. 4 January 1847, p59.

EDWIN SMITH

Wife - Mary W. Smith. Children - Franklin T., Mary Jane, Arabella H., Selina Smith. Executor - wife Mary. Witnesses - M. W. Whitehead and Willis Burton. Slaves - Sam, Ben, Lidia. 17 February 1846, p60

WILLIAM BLAKE

Wife - Agness Blake. Daughters - Jane Oneal Blake, Mary A. Foster, Sarah F. Blake, Susan E. Blake. Sons - Edward H. Blake, John Henry Blake. Executors - wife Agness and son

John Henry. Witnesses - B. F. Hundon, J. D. Calhoun, J. A. Avent. Slaves - Ben and his wife Hanner, Sam and his wife Lucy, Little Sam, Matilda, Harriott, Mary, Burrel, Phill, Mary, Peter, Rose, Louisa, Elick, Tony, Lewis, Martha, Bob, Fanny, Emily. 22 October 1846, p60.

WILLIAM THOMPSON

Wife mentioned but not named. Son - Josiah Thompson. Daughters - Mary Ann Barnes, Susan Pitman, wife of Caswell D. Pitman, Absalla Thompson, Meoly Thompson, Louisa Caveners, wife of Joab Caveners. Executor - Henry P. Barnes and son Josiah Thompson. Witnesses - Francis A. Allen, Joseph Brown, Caswell D. Pittman. Slaves - Willis, Blackwell, Fillis, Dennis, Nelson, Jefferson, Charry, Granville, Martha. Probated 3 April 1848, p62.

MARMADUKE D. KIMBROUGH

Wife - Eliza Ann Kimbrough. Five children mentioned but not named. Brother - Orman L. Kimbrough. Executors - Orman Kimbrough and William Cothran. Witnesses - Bethany Hall, W. C. Harrell, John M. Hollingsworth. 14 May 1848, p63.

JOHN D. BIBB

Sons - William C. Bibb, Dandridge A. Bibb, Algenon S. Bibb. Daughters - Laura A. Bibb, Alvira Antionette Malone, deceased. Grandaughters - Ellen Selwin and Antionette Malone, children of dec'd. daughter Alvira Antionette Malone. Grandson - John D. Bibb, son of Wm. C. Bibb. Executors - William C. Bibb, Danridge A. Bibb, Algenon Bibb. Witnesses - William Sykes, James M. Watt, W. G. Tidwell. Slaves - Patrick to be set free, James son of Julia. 24 April 1848, p65.

DRURY COMPTON

Wife - Jane Compton. Son - Allen Compton. Other children mentioned but not named. Executor - friend Allen Gary. Witnesses - D. M. Lipscomb, John Nunnery, James Jones. 13 May 1848, p67.

JOHN GARY

Daughters - Peggy Jenkins and Pernelia Harris, dec'd. Sons - Allen Gary, Marvel M. Gary, West Gary. Daughters-in-law - Betsy Gary, wife of son West; Judith W. Gary, wife of son Allen. Grandchildren - Mary Jane Gary, William West Gary, and Eliza Letitia Gary, children of son Allen. Executor - Allen Gary. Witnesses - D. M. Lipscomb, Martin Nelms, William Barrow. Slaves - Bill and his wife Judy, Emit, Andy (9 years), Ann (8 years), Ephraim (8 years), Catharine (7 years), Washington (5 years), John (4 years), Mary (4 years), Margaret (3 years), Lewis (1 year), Wilshire, Rody, Shadrack, Lear. 6 February 1843, p69.

M. I. LOCKHART

Wife - Lucinda Lockhart. Son - Samuel T. Lockhart. Brother - Thomas B. Lockhart. Nieces - Nancy Lucinda Red, wife of Dr. James W. Red; Leonona Ebins Lockhart, daughter of Thomas B. Lockhart, Ann Eliza Williams, daughter of Dr. S. I. Williams. Executor - friend Dr. James W. Red. Witnesses - T. C. Harris, W. C. Stovall, W. H. Harris. Slaves - Orange and his wife Amy, Isham, Peter and his wife Dicy, Allen, Harriet, George, Leatha. 2 February 1849, p72.

MRS. ADALINE A. PATTON

Daughter - Leonora Patton. Friend Samuel Hart to be guardian of son David Rufus. Friend Joseph Drake to be guardian of son Augustus C. Executor - Joseph Drake. Witnesses - Martha M. Drake and Joseph Swain. 14 April 1849. Probated - September 1849, p74.

WILLIAM ROBINSON

Wife - Violet S. Robinson. Witnesses - John Moffet, John Lancaster, John R. Ford. 1 August 1849. Probated - October 1849, p76.

MICAJAH T. PURNELL

(Of Knox County, Tennessee.) Sons - John H., Micajah F., Martin A. and James C. Daughters - Elizabeth H. and Eliza R. Requested that all children be college educated. Executors - Brother, Henry M. Purnell, Frank Hawkins and G. F. Neill, all of Carroll County, Mississippi. Witnesses - Robert D. Cox and H. Baker. 26 August 1849, p76.

GEORGE WASHINGTON MEEKS

(Of New Orleans.) Brothers - James H. Meeks, Thos. I. Meek, Francis Marin Meek. Six sisters mentioned but not named except for Mary. Executor - James H. Meeks. Witnesses - Thos. B. Lee, Garland Ried, Jno. McDougall, Wm. Crockett, A. A. Jones, Rich'd. McConnell. Slave - Jim Crow. 19 March 1850, p78.

WM. H. HARRIS

Brother - Thomas W. Harris (of Halifax County, North Carolina). Children - Thomas Whitman Harris and Sarah Price Harris. Sister - Rosana Branch. Executors - Thomas W. Harris and James H. Avera. Witnesses - Frank Hawkins, S. C. Gerin, S. T. Lane. 8 July 1850, p79.

S. C. GEREN

(Nuncupative will.) Statement - John P. Turner stated that Doct. Geren told him on his death bed that he wished all his property to go to his wife. He died the 19th of July, 1850. Witnesses - Jane V. Turner and Mary E. Turner, p81. (Note: Gerenton Cemetery, Carroll County, Mississippi, Simeon C. Geren, 19 July 1850, died at age 42 years 5 months.)

JOEL H. PATE

(Nuncupative will.) Spoken in the presence of A. Pate and others - "I wish Margaret to have this plantation and house, and ten negroes." No dates, p81.

VADEN HAMILTON

Near relative - Joseph P. Hughes. Friends - Joseph J. Wood, Christopher Hollinsworth, John G. Harris, John C. Hick, John D. Wiat, Christopher Gillespie, A. J. Paxton, Jeremiah Cooper, Felix G. Hiatt. Executors - Jos. P. Hughes and Joseph J. Wood. Witnesses - S. B. Bagley, Malohn D. Hackett. 2 September 1847, p81.

DR. SAMUEL D. ALEXANDER

Wife - Anna Alexander. Sons - Charles B., Dabney O., Samuel S., George W., Joseph, Thomas, Solon, Sicinjus. Daughter - Elizabeth Ann. Executors - Anna Alexander and Dabney D. Alexander. Witnesses - James Collins, Sam'l. Hart, E. S. Wellons, W. R. Russell. Slaves - Lucy and her four children, Mary, Tempe, Jacob, Hester. 4 October 1849, p82.

JAMES A. EVERETT

(Of Houston County, Georgia.) Wife - Mary Beaufort. Sons - James A. and Henry Peter. Daughters - Sarah E., Ann E., Theodosia. Brother - Charles Everett. Sisters - Nancy Furlow deceased, Patsey Bynum (her son Susan or Susars Bynum - Trustee). Nephews - George C. Everett, Tenner C. Everett, James M. Everett, Charles N. Everett. Mother-in-law - Mrs. Sarah W. Kaislor. Brothers-in-law - William Green, Peter B. Green, Miles S. Green. Sister-in-law - Elizabeth Green.

Bequeaths to Rev. Reuben H. Luckey, Charaty Harrell, Sarah Harrell, Mrs. Mary Matthews (widow of Isham Matthews). Old friends - Rev'd. James Dunwoody, Rev'd. John Fulwood. Executors - Turner C. Everett, Myles S. Green, Adolphus D. Kendrick. Witnesses - Hardy Hunter, W. H. Hollenshead, Allen Wiggins. Slaves - Early, Caroline, Burrell, Tatnall, Jerry. 8 May 1848, p83.

MARTHA C. BURTON

Son - Edward R. Burton. Daughters - Lucy Ann Moss and Martha M. Drake. Granddaughter - Martha Eliza Burton, daughter of Edward R. Burton. Grandson - Albert Drake. Executor - Edward R. Burton. Witnesses - W. M. Stansbury, Saml. Hart. Slaves - Ephraim, Davy, Henry, Stephen, Ben, Fanny, Celia Ann. 13 July 1850, p93.

GEORGE PEEBLES

(Of Halifax, North Carolina.) Sons - William, John. Daughters - Martha Drake, Mary Neville, Susan Powell, Judith, Rebecca, Prescilla, Lucy. Son-in-law - Cullen Powell. Executor - friend Thomas Ously. Witnesses - B. S. Stubbs and L. Gary. Slaves - Rhoda, Anthony, Clarey, Peter, Hannah, Guilford, Sam, Mary, Tilla, Henry, Clairborne, Fanny, Selia, Jacob, David, Creesy, Rose, Harriett, Allen, Chand. Probated August 1838, p95.

LEROY BREWER

(Nuncupative will.) Wife - Serena (present wife). Children of first wife mentioned but not named. Executor - Asbury C. Huffner. Leroy Brewer died 17 August 1851. Witnesses - Albert B. Harris, Josiah W. Hill. Slaves - Mariah, Ephraim. 25 August 1851, p97.

MRS. REBECCA ANN BLACKMON

Sons - Hezekiah Zackariah, Henry Claybourn, Thomas, Nathan, George Blackmon. Husband - Zachariah Blackman. Witnesses - Jesse Johnson, W. D. Thomason, Lydia Thomason. Slaves - Sarah (about 30), Jim (about 9), Anthony (about 6), Jinny (about 4), Betsy (about 2). 5 October 1851, p98. (Note: Blackmonton Cemetery, Carroll County, Mississippi; Rebecca Stout Blackmon, 1814-1851, wife of Zachariah and mother of five; Zachariah "Dr. Zack" Blackmon, 1811-1886, rural medicine man, merchant, planter, lay preacher.)

NATHANIEL R. FORD

Wife - Eliza Ford. Youngest children - Benjamin Franklin, William Hardiman, Simon. Other children mentioned but not named. Witnesses - Thos. S. Gardner, I. I. Dorsey, C. C. Maxwell. 26 August 1851, p99.

GRANBURY BLOUNT

Sons - Jasper & Newton Blount. Wife - Sarah Blount. Witnesses - J. W. Halley, M. Taylor. 21 March 1846, p100.

RICHARD CAMPBELL

Wife - Bertha Campbell. Daughters - Nancy Miers, Polly Ezell, Dicy Ann Jarvier. Sons - John, Jesse A. and Rich'd M. Campbell. Step-son - William T. Davis. Susan Davis mentioned. Witnesses - Ferdinand Bibb, B. F. Bibb, James F. Bibb. 31 July 1844, p101.

PLUMMER W. SMITH

Brothers - Thomas M. Smith, Robert T. Smith. Sisters - Louisa Turner, Tabatha Heath. Executor - Thomas M. Smith. Witnesses - G. A. Graves, Geo. Hightower, William Hightower. 13 May 1852, p102.

MARY E. WILDS

Brother - Robert Emmitt Merriweather. Children mentioned but not named. Witnesses - Samuel Long, James Collins. 10 May 1852, p103.

BAKER LIPSCOMB

Daughter - Lucinda Hill, wife of Abram M. Hill. Wife mentioned but not named. Executors - Abner Reeves, Abram M. Hill. Slaves - Wilson, Cina, Manda, James. Witnesses - C. O. King, Abram Hill. 17 July 1852, p103.

WILLIAM LAGRONE

Sons - Andrew, David, William. Daughters - Francis, Elizabeth McMath. Executor - Andrew Lagrone. Witnesses - William Bassett, A. H. McCorkle. Slave - Bele. 28 August 1852, p104.

EDMOND GREER

Wife - Frances Greer. Children - Asel Greer, Bingum Greer, Mary Perkins, Elizabeth Greer, Matilda Bell, Jane Randle, Lucy Ann Gordon, Franky Murphy, Edmond P. Greer (youngest). Children of Mary Perkins - Duster, Thomas, Mary, Leonidas, Henrietta. Danl. D. Murphy trustee for

Perkins children. Executors - Thom. J. Fulliton and Dan'l. D. Murphy. Witnesses - Robert Eakin, William Beatty, Thom. J. Fulliton. Slaves - Sawry, Jack, Lucinda and her child Catharine, Maranda, Frank. 30 August 185?, p105.

ABRAM HILL

Wife - Clorissa Hill. Children - Josiah W. Hill, John W. Hill, Sarah A. Reeves, William G. Hill, Abram W. Hill, Eli Hill, Henry W. Hill. Allen G. Hill's children mentioned but not named. Executors - Abner Reeves and Josiah W. Hill. Witnesses - Abram Hill, Eli Hill. 26 June 1849. Addition signed 27 September 1852, p106.

WILLIAM COATS

Wife - Susan C. Coats. Brother - Moses B. Coats. Witnesses - John B. Heath, B. Latham, Allen Rodgers. 14 September 1852, p107.

SUSAN R. COUGER

Children - Benjamin N. and Edward L. Couger. Sisters - Nancy Neal and E. D. Holmes. Brother - Wm. D. Neal of Rutherford County, Tennessee. Mentioned - Wm. L. Couger and Sarah Couger. Witnesses - I. A. Godfrey, L. M. Holmes, S. T. Land, S. Atchison. Executor - Stephen Johnson. 29 September 1852, p108.

JESSE B. STEDMAN

(Nuncupative will.) Daughters - Louisiana M. Stedman, Mary E. Stedman. Son - Hibbard Stedman. Testimony given by Pleasant Merrill. Mentioned - H. A. Reynolds. Witnesses - W. S. Pullen and James S. Pentecost. Money owed by Jesse Reed. Probated - 2 May 1855, p109.

SAMUEL MEEK

Wife - Jestiana Meek. Brother - James Meek. Executor - James Meek. Witnesses - Robt. Meek, Joseph Meek. Slave - Citty. 15 July 1833, p109.

REUBEN GAYDEN

Wife - Jane Gayden. Children - William A. Gayden and Susannah Elizabeth Booth. Younger children mentioned but not named. Step-children - Alphonzo and Greenwood Hearns. Friends - William Booth, David Holman. Witnesses - James R. Lowrie, Jesse G. Duren. 15 July 1850. Addition dated 19 May 1853. Witnesses - J. W. Dismukes, H. A. Reynolds, p110.

RICHARD A. TOWNES

Wife - E. A. C. Townes (formerly E. A. C. Seight). Brother - Robert I. Townes. Sister-in-law - Patter C. Townes (formerly Patter C. Eggleston), wife of Robert I. Townes of Brazoria County, State of Texas. Witnesses - M. Conley, E. L. McCracken, T. L. Burges. Executor - John A. Binford. 9 June 1851, p111.

ELIZABETH CHEEK

Youngest son - Eli Cheek. Other children mentioned but not named. Witnesses - Jno. E. Palmer, W. T. Collier, Henry Pitman. 5 May 1853, p112.

PETER E. REDDITT

Wife - Olivia Redditt. Children mentioned but not named. Witnesses - S. S. Price and A.. L. Redditt. 1 June 1853, p113.

ABRAM M. HILL

Wife and children mentioned but not named. Executor - Brother - Henry W. Hill. Witnesses - A. Reeves, Thos W. Beck, Josiah W. Hill. 6 December 1853, p113.

JOHN S. PEED

Wife - Olivia Peed. Daughter - Sarah Elizabeth. Mother - Elizabeth Peed. Father-in-law - Lodoniah Redditt. Bequeaths to - Sydney Smaw, Edward Smaw, Henry Smaw, William E. Smaw, John Warren, Elizabeth Warren, William Warren, Alva D. Warren. Executor - friend Will B. Rodman. Witnesses - Peter G. Yates and Will B. H. Garard. Slaves - Anonas, Winny, Dolly, Phoebe, Jarvis, Delsey, Ned, Caesar, Moses, Simon, Jim, Reuben, Elsy, Edy, Jane. 10 December 1843. Probated - March 1844, Beauford County, North Carolina, p114.

JANE G. FRAZIER

Brothers - Thomas G. Frazier, Ephraim Frazier, Sylvanus I. Frazier. Mother - Jane G. Frazier. Sister - Lucinda Frazier. Nephew - Mitton Frazier, son of Ephraim Frazier. Cousin - Ephraim Frazier. Executor - Felix L. Herring. Witnesses - Saml. Hart, Saml. B. Jones, Joshua Whitmore. Slaves - Violet and her son Nicholas. 29 May 1847, p116.

MRS. ELIZABETH MURDOCK

Sons - William M. Murdock, Alfred Murdock. Daughter -

Margaret H. Bacon. Grandchildren - Harriet Coleman, Louisa Bacon and Allan Bacon. Executor - William D. Thomason. Witnesses - Samuel Buffkin, W. D. Thomason. Slaves - Mary (aged 20), Anny (aged about 4), Betsey (aged about 40), Wiate (aged about 15), Milly (aged about 11), George (aged about 5). 6 May 1852. Probated 6 March 1854, p117. (Note: Margaret Coleman married James F. Bacon, Carroll County, Mississippi, 18 December 1842.)

FRANKLIN M. STEVENS

Wife - Caroline Stevens. Witnesses - S. B. Arnold, T. Morgan Smith, Ephraim Hoover. Slave - Fillis. 21 March 1854, p118.

ROBERT TURNER

(Nuncupative will.) Wife - Adaliza Turner. Daughter - Eliza Medora Almeia Turner. Mentioned child to be born. Witnesses - James Standley, Jr. and Samuel J. Hood. 23 April 1854, p119.

ELIJAH SULLIVAN

Sons - T. W. Sullivan, A. J. Sullivan, William N. Sullivan. Daughters - Sarah Angelina Sullivan, Elizabeth Denman, Julia Ann Denman. Executor - T. W. Sullivan. Witnesses - B. F. Sanders, Hardey Bennett, Sampson W. Holland, J. Z. George. Slaves - Saline, Dilla, Smith, Cynthia, Steven. 24 February 1854, p119.

MISS A. ADELAIDE GEREN

Father - Abram Geren. Mother - Sarah Ann Geren. Sisters - Sarah Ann M'Lemore, Mary A. Geren. Brothers - Wm. P. Tyson, Aaron L. Tyson. Brother-in-law - John D. M'Lemore. Executor - John D. M'Lemore. Witnesses - W. W. Liddell, A. L. Tyson. Slaves - Nancy, Mary Jane, Neck, Veney. 30 July 1854, p112. (Note: Gerenton Cemetery, Carroll County, Mississippi, A. Adelaide Geren, 25 September 1831 - 7 August 1854.)

ROBERT B. KINKADE

Wife - Ferely Ann Kinkade. Executor - George Scarlet. Daughter - Bonetta Arabella. Witnesses - U. Stancill, Asa Bales, Robert C. Hargrove. 15 May 1850. Probated - 4 September 1854, p123.

JOHN BASKIN, SR.

Bequeaths to grandchildren - four children of James A. Baskins, four children of Wm. C. Baskins, three children of Isabella R. Hawthorn, three children of Margaret Ann Staten, four children of John H. Baskins, John A. Baskin, son of James C. Baskin. Heirs of Drusilla McFarland mentioned. Friend - John McCorkle. Witnesses - I. F. Sanders, A. H. McCorkle, I. M. Thomson. 12 September 1854, p124.

HOWELL ADAMS

Son - Henry M. Adams. Wife - Elmira Adams. Infant Daughter - Mary Emma Adams. George W. Vanhook mentioned. Executor - Elmira Adams. Witnesses - Wm. A. McCain, David Long, Wm. L. Meux. Slaves - Moses, Angelina, Amanda and her child Heary, Myra. 5 December 1854, p125.

GRAFTON GATEWOOD

Wife - Elizabeth Gatewood. Sister - Lucy Woodell. Witnesses - C. C. Hight, David Blount, G. A. Spivey. Slaves - Hannah, Jefferson, Joseph, John, Amy. 16 September 1854. Probated - April 1855, p126.

CHARLES P. SHEPPARD

Sisters - Matilda Caldwell, Mary A. Hurt. Brother-in-law - A. S. Caldwell. Nephew - A. O. P. Nicholson, Jr. Bequeaths to - Mrs. Elizabeth Condit, Albert Drake, John Drake (sons of friend Capt. J. Drake). Mentioned - Friend A. W. Ayres, Doctor E. R. McLean, Mother's grave at Nashville, Sister's grave at Memphis. Executors - A. S. Caldwell, Capt. Joseph Drake. Witnesses - Silas Condit, Angus W. Ayres, W. B. Helm. Slave - Gim. 12 March 1855, p127.

JOHN HOLMAN

Sons - Elijah Holman Jesse Holman, Nathaniel Holman. Granddaughter - Caroline (daughter of Thomas Holman). Bequeath to children of Amos Holman. Executors - Jesse, Nathaniel & Elijah Holman. Witnesses - Simon T. Turner, James E. Lott, Jackson Leflore. 2 November 1853. Probated - April 1855, p129.

JOHN STOVALL

Daughters - Lanizer Hight, Sarah Furguson, Mary Spivy, Eveline Margaret Stovall. Sons - Wm. P. Stovall, David G. Stovall, Lewis A. Stovall. Executors - Sons David and Lewis. Witnesses - Josiah Ratliff, A. C. Stovall, W. N. Hurt. Slaves - Eliza, Laura, Manerva, Lucy. 15 November 1855. Probated - December 1855, p131.

GEORGE W. WIGGINS

(Nuncupative will.) Made at residence of B. F. Jones. Spoken to Wilson Aldridge. Mentioned - Elijah McMath, Mother (unnamed), an Isabell. Witnesses - W. M. Aldridge, ? H. O'Neal, J. J. Beck, B. F. Jones, S. J. Frazier. 22 October 1855, p133.

EUGENE A. KENNEDY

Mother - Frances A. Kennedy. Executor - Frances A. Kennedy. Witnesses - William M. Holland, F. A. Pleasants, E. L. Wad. 4 January 1853, p134.

WILLIAM W. GATES

(Nuncupative will.) Testimony of Augustus C. Rose. Bequeath to John W. Gates of South Lowell, Orange County, North Carolina. Witnesses - A. C. Rose, M. J. Rose. 24 February 1856, p135.

AARON LOTT

Son - John Lott. Children and grandchildren mentioned but not named. Witnesses - O. L. Kimbrough, Jonathan Durdin. Executor - John Lott. 11 May 1853. Probated - August 1856, p135.

TRUMAN HELTON

Wife - Mary. Witnesses - R. E. Meriwether, Wm. L. Meux, R. T. Bumsed. 6 August 1856, p137.

ELIJAH HOLMAN

(Nuncupative will.) Made at residence of Mrs. Ann G. Holman. Brother-in-law - Mr. Brown. Children mentioned but not named. Witnesses - W. W. Hart, Jas. M. Ray, A. A. McFessan. 1 August 1856. Probated - 6 Oct. 1856, p138

TITUS HOWARD

Sons - Lewis T. Howard, John T. A. Howard. Daughter - Louisa Moore. Granddaughters - Mary Louisa Howard, Olive Howse, Martha Susan Slamons. Daughter-in-law - Ann Howard. Mentioned - Louisa Ann, Rosanna Thrasher, Mary Henry, Anna Maria, Sally Barret, Edmon Florance Howard, children of Ann Howard, and Stephen B. Arnold. Executors - John T. A. Howard, Lewis T. Howard, and Louisa Moore. Witnesses - James Blanks, A. W. Bartlett, Eli Oneal, G. W. Townsend. Slaves - Hannah & Sophia to be freed, Yellow George. Probated - November 1856, p140. (Note: Howard Cemetery, Carroll County, Mississippi - Titus Howard 12

March 1785 - 12 Oct 1856, Mary Gray wife of Titus Howard 30 July 1785 - 30 July 1850.)

JESSE G. DUNN

Wife & children mentioned but not named. Witnesses - B. B. Bird, James Merrill. 26 February 1855. Probated - 3 February 1857, p142.

LOUISA McNEILL

Mentioned - Neal McNeill, heirs of Wm. McNeill, Hector McNeill, heirs of John McNeill, Louisa McNeill, Louisa Sinclair, James McNeill. Executor - Isaac Sullivan. Witnesses - J. J. Andrews, H. G. Bennett. Slaves - Lotty, Columbice, Peter. 23 February 1857, p143. Testimony followed by Dr. Sullivan, family physician.

WILLIAM KIRKWOOD

Wife - Rachel Kirkwood. Daughter - Narcissa Hudson, wife of Alfred Hudson. Neice - Ann Newman, wife of James V. Newman. Executor - Rachel Kirkwood. Witnesses - W. Cothran, W. B. Helm, Chas. Kopperl. Slaves - Andrew, Sharlette & her child S. S. Prestin. 13 June 1856. Probated - November 1858, p146. (Note: Narcissa Kirkwood married Alfred Hudson 11-15-1848.)

JOHN CARPENTER

Wife - Easter Carpenter. Witnesses - Wm. Carpenter, Owen Carpenter. S. Atchison. Slaves - Tony, Liza. 26 January 1857. Probated - July 1857, p147.

SEABORN JONES

Wife mentioned but not named. Daughter - Nancy Ann Ammons. Son - John M. Jones. Bequeaths to - Reuben Jones, Seaborn Jones, Patrick H. Jones and Emily Jones. Witnesses - B. H. Wellons, Chas. P. Sheppard, R. W. Williamson. 8 May 1854. Probated - August 1857, p148.

WILLIAM A. McMATH

Wife & children mentioned but not named. Executor - friend Robert Neal, Sr. Witnesses - John A. Binford, Chesley Holloway, Nancy E. Holloway. Probated - August 1857, p149.

JOSEPH MEEK KEYS

Wife - Ann Elizabeth Keys. Nephew - Joseph M. Keys, Jr. Executors - Sairtes J. Keys, Albert G. Keys, Francis W.

Keys. Witnesses - John D. McLemore, R. N. Perkins, N. T. Durham. 25 July 1857. Probated - Sept. 1857, p151.

SARAH KIRBY

Daughters - Elizabeth P. Hoy, Susan A. Kirby, Nancy F. Sabin, Sarah E. Kirby, Rebecca T. Kirby. Son - Albert M. Kirby. Executor - Albert M. Kirby. Witnesses - Willis B. Smith, J. A. Applewhite, T. W. Vanse. Slaves - Sarah and her three children: Caroline, Mary, and Harrett. 3 September 1856. Probated - October 1857, p152.

THOMAS HARVEY

Wife - Precilla Harvey. Witnesses - C. C. Ratliff, H. B. Latham, P. E. Holmes. Slaves - Anderson and wife Phillis and their daughter Caroline, Allen, Louis, Squire, Angeline, Salina, Cela, Lucinda. 7 September 1857. Probated - 2 Nov. 1857, p154.

WILLIAM Y. BELER

Wife - Elizabeth B. Beler. Executor - William P. Fisackerly. Witnesses - C. D. Pitman, M. L. Beler. Slave - Caroline. 13 August 1857, p156. (Note: W. Y. Beler married Eliza B. Holmes 24 Dec. 1849.)

JESSE HEATH

Son - Henry Heath. Executor - Henry Heath. Witnesses - J. Z. George, R. W. Williamson, Saml. Moore. 2 September 1857, p158.

ALLEN TURRENTINE

Wife - Martha L. Turrentine. Children mentioned but not named. Executor - Martha L. Turrentine. Witnesses - C. M. Vaiden, T. C. Everett, Frank Hawkins. 23 October 1857. Probated - December 1857, p159.

J. B. COHRON

Wife - Jane Cohron. Heirs - John B. Cohron, Cornelius H. Cohron. Brothers - David H. Cohron, James Cohron. Executors - David H. Cohron, James Cohron. Witnesses - Frank Hawkins, Wm. Mattox, J. M. Hamilton. 21 January 1858. Probated - 9 March 1858, p161. (Note: John Butler Cohron married Jane Garland 11 Sept. 1853. Headstone at New Salem Cemetery, Carroll County: John B. Cohron 9-14-1818 2-9-1858.)

A. O. WINN

Wife - Ann J. Winn. Nephews - A. J. Winn, Oliver Winn Phillip. Bequeaths to - Mrs. Ann Gadberry, Miss Jane Atchison, James Atchison, Sarah A. Gadberry. Executors - Ann J. Winn and Samuel Atchison. Slaves - April and his wife Adiline, Sam Slick and his wife Felicity, Washington, Rafe, Phillis. 21 January 1858. Probated - 8 June 1858, p163. (Note: Augustus O. Winn married Ann Jane Pate 8-27-1850.)

HENRY SHERIN

Wife - Ann Mariah Sherin. Daughter - Mary Ann Sykes. Mentioned - Joel Sherin. Witnesses - J. Sullivan, J. C. Aden, Hollis H. Williams. 12 December 1857. Probated 5 May 1858, p163.

LEE (LEO?) TAYLOR

Wife - Agness A. Taylor. Children - (these were very faint and difficult to read) Nancy Mims/Nelms, Camah Bennth, Caroline McArley, Leo Taylor, Menisz Taylor, dec'd, Perwilly Bennett, dec'd, George Taylor, Hesster A. Far. Executors - Son Leo and wife Agness. Slave - Marino. 24 August 1858, p164.

REV. JOSEPH TRAVIS

Wife mentioned but not named. Wife's parents - John & Polly Butler (both dec'd.). Friend - Rev. M. J. Blackwell. Nephews - Rev. Tracy R. Walsh (of Ansou County, North Carolina) and Jos. Travis Walsh (of Conwayboro P. O., South Crolina). Neices - B. Cunningham (of Gold Hill P. O., North Carolina), Nancy C. Nesbitt (of Montroall P. O., Missouri), and Olive W. Clark (of Marion P. O., Ohio). Bequeaths to - Jos. Travis Graves, son of G. A. Graves, and Joseph Travis Rohr (of Harrisonburg, Virginia). Mentioned - Rev. E. W. Lehon, D. D. Executor - friend R. D. McLane (of Grenada, Yalobusha County, Mississippi). Witnesses - W. S. Beauchamp, Henry C. Edgar, P. M. Miller. Slaves - Stephen, Ann, Lizzy, Letha, Sterling, Martha, Buttons, Charlotte and her son Josiah, Charles. 6 August 1858. Codicil - request he be buried under the pulpit at Spring Hill Church. Probated 6 Oct. 1858, p167.

A. B. ROBINSON

Wife - Nancy Robinson. Sons - Jeremiah Robinson and Douglass Robinson. Executors - wife & two sons. Witnesses - John Ray, L. Velina Mitchell, Jeremiah S. Robinson, Smith L. Young. 8 October 1858. Probated - Jan. 1859, p170.

H. H. WEIR

Wife and children mentioned but not named. Executor - Wife. Witnesses - T. C. Harris, Lucinda Lockhart, F. P. Pleasants. 6 July 1857. Filed - 4 January 1859, p172.

SAMUEL T. LOCKHART

Wife- Ophelia Lockhart. Daughter - Ella C. Lockhart. Mother - Lucinda Lockhart (of Holmes County, Mississippi). Mentioned - Andrew Oldham. Executors - Lucinda Lockhart and J. W. Rėd. Witnesses - Thos. C. Harris, Saml. S. Brown, Zen Oldham. Slaves - Harriett and her three children Ben, Adeline, and infant Evelinor; Andy, Lairsah, Leah, Fred, George, Leatha, Caroline, Sane, Mary, Isham, Ann, Bill, Allen. November 29, 1858, p174.

JOSIAH M. BAGLEY

Wife - Huldah Bagley. Witnesses - S. M. McClurg, Y. C. McClurg, D. Davis. 16 March 1859. Probated 4 April 1859, p177.

RICHARD BUCKLEY

Wife and children mentioned but not named. 13 December 1858. Probated - March 1859, p178.

WILLIAM PEEBLES

Sister - Mary R. Sledge. Neices - Mary E. Sledge & Susan R. Sledge. Nephews - John H. Sledge & Albert R. Sledge. Brother-in-law - George M. Sledge. Executor - George M. Sledge. Witnesses - Thos. Allen, W. A. Swift, E. E. Foltz. Slaves - Alsey (about 12), Rose (about 15), Harriett, Eliza, Julia. 7 October 1857. Probated - 4 April 1859, p179.

JEFFERSON C. PATE

Wife - Eliza F. Pate. Children - S. Fannie Pate, George Pate, Lilly Pate, Bloom Pate, (deceased - Anna, Lilla & Charles Henderson). Witnesses - W. W. Glenn, A. Pate. February 1859. Probated - May 1859, p181. Requested he be buried by his deceased children. (Note: J. C. Pate married E. F. Smith 2-22-1848.)

WILSON HEMINGWAY

Neice - Margaret Daniel. Deceased neice - Elizabeth Woodbing, sister of Margaret Daniel. Brothers - William Hemingway, Collins F. Hemingway. Executors - William & Collins F. Hemingway. Slaves - Yanaky, Martha, Peyton,

Gilbert, Armstead, Charles, Benton (called Monkey). 22 November 1858. Probated - May 1859, p182.

ANNANIAN PATE

Sons - (eldest) Joel Henderson Pate, (2nd) James Dunlap Pate, (3rd) Jefferson Charles Pate. Daughter - Ann Jane Winn. Wife mentioned but not named. Granddaughter - Mary H. Pate. Executors - sons James and Jefferson. Witnesses - S. Atchison, S. T. Clement, D. O. Alexander. Slaves - Rubin, Frank, Harrison, Yellow Mary, Sarah Ann, Big John, Maria, Ira, Riller, L. Ben, Caroline, Martha, B. Ben, Margaret Ann, Gincy, Gun Polk, George, General, Mitchel, Alvira, Perry. 13 Jan. 1844. Probated - August 1859, p184. (Note: Joel H. Pate married M. S. Conner 4-25-1848.)

CHESLEY HOLLOWAY

Wife - Nancy Emeline Holloway. Children mentioned but not named. Executor - friend Robert Neal Sr. Witnesses - A. C. Hendren, E. H. Edmondson, Sion Horn. 25 January 1859. Probated 1 August 1859, p186.

JESSE C. MOHEAD

(Nuncupative will.) Wife - Rachel Mohead. Children mentioned but not named. Witnesses - Dr. John W. Sanders, William Mohead, Aaron Lott. 29 June 1859. Probated 6 Sept. 1859, p188.

ALFRED MOORE

Wife - Rachel Moore. Grandchildren - James Monroe Moore, Sarah Frances Moore, Rachel Rebecca Moore, Alfred David Moore, Mary Walker Moore, William Nesbet Moore. Daughter-in-law - Mary W. Moore. Executor - Rachel Moore. Friends - J. G. Adaire, W. J. Herring. 12 May 1859. Filed - 8 November 1859, p188.

ABRAHAM GEREN

Wife - Sarah Ann Geren. Children - Eliza C. Bethel, Mary E. Gibson, Hetty E. Davis, Sarah A. McLemore. Executors - John D. McLemore, John H. Davis. Witnesses - H. A. Reynolds, James C. Wright, Ausley McCarroll. 5 May 1857. Probated - November 1859, p190.

WM. P. GUNN

(Nuncupative will.) Wife - Caroline E. Gunn. Children mentioned but not named. Executors & Witnesses - Jack Moore, Wm. A. McCain, N. H. McCain. 15 October 1859, p191.

JOHN LITTLE

Nephews - George Little, son of brother Wm. Little, and Edmund Little, son of dec'd. brother E. P. Little of North Carolina. Sisters - Elizabeth S. Dunn, wife of James B. Dunn of South Carolina and Nancy D. Baucum, wife of Alfred Baucum. Executor - William C. Eskridge, A. D. Greene. Witnesses - J. A. J. Askew, S. F. Marsh, John A. Fox. Slave - Peter. 3 January 1860, p193.

ELIJAH McMATH

Daughter - Margaret Emma. Other children mentioned but not named. Executor - C. C. Campbell. Witnesses - J. W. Wall, Duncan Evans, W. Z. Spruell. 2 Octoter 1859. Filed - 6 February, 1860

GEORGE BAMBURG

Property to be kept together for the use of his wife and children, unnamed. Wife and children to manage property. Witnesses - B. B. Love and Thomas B. Weed. 16 March 1860, p199.

JORDAN MORRIS

Wife - Martha Morris. Son - John Morris. Mentions other children, unnamed. Executor - John Morris. Witnesses - James E. Lott, Aaron Lott Jr., B. J. Lott. 25 December 1858. Probated - 19 June 1860, p201.

GEORGE W. SLEDGE

Wife - Sarah Sledge. Children mentioned but not named. Brother - Joseph Sledge. Executor - Joseph Sledge. Witnesses - C. C. Campbell, E. H. Edmonson, Joseph W. Comfort. May 1860. Filed - 18 July 1860, p202.

MRS. LOUISA MOORE

Husband - Saml. Moore. Brothers - Edward Howard dec'd., Louis Howard, John Howard. Bequeaths to - Louisa Ann Howard, Rosanns Thrasher Howard, Mary Henry Howard, Ann Mariah Howard, Sally Burnet Howard, Edward Florence Howard. Children - L. Henry T. Moore, Mary Lucinda Moore, William Robert Moore. Witnesses - J. Z. George, J. W. Sinclair. 28 July 1855. Probated - October 1860, p203.

RICHARD ESKRIDGE

Son - Tallifairo Eskridge. Daughters - Rebecca Weed, wife

of Cooper Weed; and Mary A. Smith. Bequeaths to - Julia Eskridge, widow of Thos. Eskridge; and Julia A. Bamburg. Executors - John A. Binford, Robt. Neal Sr., and grandson Burditt Eskridge. Witnesses - Chas. P. Sheppard, W. M. Stansbury, J. A. J. Askew, B. F. Jones. Slaves - Mosses Jr., Bill, Mitch, Rich., Martha and her son Jim, Luke and his wife Amanda and their child Nelson, Elias, Abram. 7 October 1853, p406. Codicil (p407) Brother - Saml. B. Eskridge and his wife Sophia Eskridge. 24 September 1854. Witnesses - Will Sanders, R. W. Williamson, Chas. P. Sheppard. Codicil (p408) Grandsons - Blewitt Love, B. B. Love. 9 March 1860

JAMES H. PETTYGREW

Wife - Malena Pettygrew. Sons - Lewis, William, Robert, Frank. Daughters - Mary Lew, Ellen, Amanda Alice and Della. Executor - Malena Pettygrew. Witnesses - Richard Nelson, John P. Marshall, R. J. Davis. 26 May 1860. Probated 19 Feb. 1861, p412.

JAMES W. HENRY

Sisters - Emily A. Henry, Elizabeth E. Henry, Sarah A. Henry. Witnesses - T. P. Pleasants, Saml. Hart, J. W. Nelson. 2 July 1860, p414.

ARMSTED BELER

Bequeaths to - Susan Gambel, Sarah Beler, Estell Beler, Blevins D. Beler, Armsted H. Beler, James Beler, Marcus L. Beler, William Y. Beler, Henred G. Beler (son of Wm. Y. Beler), Milton W. Beler, Asbury H. Beler, Jane T. Williams. Executor - William Crawford. Witnesses - Thos. E. Buchanan, H. P. Aikens. Slaves - Palina and her three children Grace, Matilda & Mancea, Rachel and her child Monrow, Manday. 8 June 1859, p415.

ROBERT NEAL (Sr. or Jr.)

Wife - Elmira Neal. Oldest daughter - Sarah Elizabeth Bell. Son - Stephen R. Neal. Executors - Elmira and Stephen R. Neal. Witnesses - B. B. Taylor, M. J. Rose, Y. P. Rose. Slaves - John (age 8), Mary (age 3). 1 April 1859, p416.

JAMES BLANKS

Sisters - Mary Bartlett, Elizabeth J. Blanks (of North Carolina). Nephew - William Blanks (of North Carolina). Children of Elizabeth J. Blanks - Sarah N. Blanks, Catharine H. McLann, James H. Blanks, William Blanks. Executors - R. J. Blanks and A. W. Bartlett. Witnesses - Saml. M.

Hankins, B. B. Drane, T. D. Sherman. Slaves - Barbary and her child Barbary, Lucky. 19 February 1861, p417.

R. W. MORRISON

Mother - Susannah Morrison. Sisters - Sarah Morrison and Jane Morrison (idiot). Bequeath to Lizzie Morgan, daughter of William and Lou Morgan of Marshall County, Tennessee. Mentioned - W. A. Morrison (Benton County, Arkansas), three brothers and three sisters. Brother - Rev. A. W. Morrison. Executor - Rev. A. W. Morrison. Slave - Amanda (about 25). 25 January 1859. Probated 27 May 1861, p420.

SAMUEL ATCHISON

Daughters - Sarah Ann Gadberry, Elizabeth Jane Atchison. Executors - Son-in-law M. S. Gadberry & James M. Johnson. Witnesses - James Minter, Jno. Spann, P. Runger, James M. Lynch. Slaves - Tiletha, Lucy. 5 February 1861. Probated - 19 Aug. 1861, p422.

WILLIAM E. MATTHEWS

Wife - Ann D. Matthews. Children mentioned but not named. Executor - Ann D. Matthews. Witnesses - W. W. Brewer, R. S. Matthews. 22 October 1860. Probated - 16 Sept. 1861, p425.

EZEKIEL PICKENS

Father - H. C. Pickins. Mother - Mrs. Agness Pickins. Sisters - Rebecca and Eliza. Brother - Andrew Pickens. Bequeaths to Mother, Rebecca, Eliza and Mary. Aunt - Mrs. R. Anderson. Mentioned - Mr. Moses Hubbard of Eutaw, Alabama; Mr. Jos. Pickins, Dr. T. Brown, the late Judge Pickens. Requested mother to give Tom to Molly and Hagar. Witnesses - Mary J. Pickens, A. C. Pickins. Executors - N. C. Pickins and Dr. Thomas Boon. 23 April 1861, p427.

AARON L. TYSON

(Nuncupative will.) Wife and children mentioned but not named. Witnesses - A. Woods, A. W. Gary. 22 May 1861, p429.

AMBROSE E. McMATH

Wife - Mary McMath. Owned property at Black Hawk, Mississippi. Brother - John McMath. Children mentioned but not named. Executors - Mary McMath and John McMath. Witnesses - I. F. Smith, W. H. Johnson, H. I. Reid. 14 January 1860. Probated - 19 Sept. 1861, p430.

JOSIAH NEWMAN, dec'd.

Son - James Newman. Daughters - Elizabeth Davis, wife of Genl. A. M. Davis, Francis Leflore, wife of John D. Leflore, Mary E. Young, wife of M. P. Young, Harriett E. Cocke, wife of B. W. Cocke, Lucy Ann Newman. Executor - Genl. A. M. Davis. Witnesses - H. T. Cocke, J. H. Young, I. S. Young. Slaves - Mary and her daughter Mace, Ann, Lourenna, George, Daniel, Sam, Parthena, Isabella and her brother Noble, Mary Amy and her brother Isaac, Andrew. 10 July 1860. Probated - November 1861, p432.

ELIZABETH B. SMITH

Husband - David H. Smith. Children - Lizzie, Louisa, Henry Curtis. Witnesses - T. S. Treadgill, W. D. F. Treadgill, J. H. Pate. Slaves - York, John, Jim, Charlotte, Nancy Hany, Isabell, Ben, Martha Marred, Caroline, William. 29 November 1861. Probated - January 1862, p434.

E. D. GREEN

Friend - Mary Grider, wife of C. R. Grider. Executor - friend W. C. Eskridge. Witnesses - P. W. Hemphill, Jno. Nunnery, R. M. Holeman. 26 November 1861. Probated - February 1862, p435.

PETER BUSH

Daughter - Emma A. Bush. Bequeath to Martha Vasser. Witnesses - W. H. M. McCain, Henry Tindall, N. H. McCain. Executor - Charles W. Vasser. 10 June 1861. Probated - February 1862, p436.

JAMES T. MATHEWS

Wife mentioned but not named. Executor - W. N. Scales. Witnesses - R. Ettiger, D. L. Linch, I. H. Peeples. 9 January 1862, p437.

TIMOTHY W. SULLIVAN

Wife - Eliza Sullivan. Children mentioned but not named. Executor - Eliza Sullivan. Witnesses - A. W. Bartlett, H. S. Hill, A. M. Nelson, H. N. Paine. 20 Dec. 1861. Probated - 19 March 1862, p438.

JOHN MORRIS

Wife - Mary Elizabeth Morris. Executor - Mary Elizabeth Morris. Witnesses - W. W. Liddell, Jas. E. Lott, Charles Morris. 21 May 1862, p440.

DAVID R. TURNER

Mother - Sarah Turner. Children mentioned but not named. Witnesses - Edward T. Wright, I. W. Sanders. 8 October 1861. Probated - July 1862, p442.

JOHN J. MATTHEWS

Wife - I. B. Matthews. Children mentioned but not named. Executors - I. B. Matthews and John C. McCurty. Witnesses - I. A. Askew, W. J. Woodell, D. L. Wingfield. 5 July 1862, p443.

JAMES H. PATE

(Of Corinth, Mississippi.) Wife - Henrietta Pate. 14 May 1862, p444.

AARON LOTT

Sons - James E. Lott, Benjamin J. Lott, Aaron G. Lott, John William Lott. Daughter - Margaret A. Lott. Wife - Margaret Lott. Executor - James E. Lott. Witnesses - W. W. Liddell, W. M. Stansbury, Mary E. Morris. Slaves - Gary, Bill, Green, Sophia, Abram, Mollie, Hannah. 24 April 1862, p445.

MARGARET STOVALL

Sons - William C., Newton, Jones H. Daughter - Martha Meredith. Grandson - Lewis Hardy Robinson. Executor - William C. Stovall. Witnesses - Josiah Stovall, Gabriel Hogard. 18 May 1862. Probated - August 1862, p446.

B. B. LOVE

Wife - Mary Elizabeth Love. Executor - Dr. John W. Sanders. Witnesses - John McCurry, S. T. Ferguson, William Bamberg. 14 March 1862. Probated - Nov. 1862, p448.

WILLIAM R. KING

Wife - Margaret Ann King. Children - Samuel W. King, Mary E. King, Sarah A. R. King. Executor - Margaret Ann King. Witnesses - Geo. C. Everett, W. B. Hudson. 18 October 1862. Probated - November 1862, p450.

M. T. PURNELL

Aunt - Mrs. Mary E. Kendall. Brothers - Martin A. Purnell, James C. Purnell. Sisters - Mrs. Hellen E. Foltz, Mrs. Eliza R. Sturdivant. Executors - Frank Hawkins, E. E. Foltz. Witnesses - J. M. Hamilton, J. A. McBride, Jno. C. Davis.

Slaves - Susanna, Porter, Sarah, Hudson, Tom, Malissa, Melly, John, Bill. 1 December 1862. Probated - December 1862, p451. (Note: Vaiden Cemetery, Carroll County, Mississippi: Micajah Thomas Purnell d. 3 Dec. 1862, aged 29 years, 5 mos., 16 days.)

L. W. HERRING

Wife & children mentioned but not named. Executor - Dr. C. M. Vaiden. Witnesses - Cisero Kennedy, Walter Kennedy. 24 January 1863, p453.

DEMPSEY BECKWITH

Wife mentioned but not named. Children - Nancy Margaret, Dempsey and Alexander Roy. Witnesses - M. H. McCarroll, Caswell Howard, Alexander Ray. 22 June 1861. Probated - March 1863, p454.

FIRD BIBB

Wife - Nancy H. Bibb. Children mentioned but not named. Witnesses - J. Durden, M. M. Liddell, O. L. Kimbrough. Probated - March 1863, p455.

SUSAN W. BIBB

Son - Ferdinand Bibb, dec'd. Daughter-in-law - Nancy H. Bibb. Youngest child of Nancy H. Bibb - Albert Bibb. Executor - Nancy H. Bibb. Witnesses - J. W. Sanders, J. E. Lott, M. A. E. Turner. Probated - June 1863, p456.

H. L. BENNETT

(Noncupative will.) Brother - Oliver Bennett. Bequeath to heirs of George Tyler. Witness - Michael McGinly. (Was a soldier in the Army and died at Catoosa Springs, Georgia, about the 20th August.) Probated - September 1863, p457.

William J. L. BECK

(Made at Richmond, Virginia.) Wife - Mary A. Beck. Children mentioned but not named. Witnesses - A. M. Nelson, B. F. Jones, J. C. Lott. Executor - Mary A. Beck. 23 August 1862. Probated - November 1863, p458.

JOSIAH SHARPE

Children - Sarah I. and James A. Sharpe. Executor - Wife, unnamed. Witnesses - N. H. McCain, S. B. Johnson, W. S. Lee. 18 July 1863. Probated - January 1864, p459.

WILLIAM M. SMITH

Wife - Jacky Ann Smith. Three youngest children - Henry Clay, Samuel McNair, George Washington. Son - John E. Smith. Daughter - Elizabeth Runey. Grandchildren - George Washington and Zibby Elizabeth Chapman. Witnesses - T. W. Scales, David Spells, B. R. Mayes. 10 February 1864. Probated - April 1864, p461.

ISAAC DUNN

Wife - Penelope A. Dunn. Children - Virginia L., Albert G. and Missouri C. Executor - Benjamin T. Marshall. Witnesses - M. C. Wellons, J. W. Nabors, R. Nelson. 8 March 1862. Probated - April 1864, p463.

ROBERT McNULTY

(Noncupative will.) Sisters - Isabella Vance, Polly Vance. Witness - John Lott. 16 May 1864, p464.

M. L. BELER

(Noncupative will.) Wife mentioned but not named. Witnesses - A. W. Gary, Lindsey Durham. 2 February 1864. Probated - April 1864, p465.

UPTON MONEY

Brother - Pearson Money. Son - William Cothran Money. Executor - Pearson Money. Witness - James S. Johnson. 1 December 1863. Probated 20 June 1864, p465.

NEWTON HARBIN

Wife - Mary Harbin. Sons - Alfred and William Maberry. Deceased daughters - Lucinda Julina Holland and Nancy Colvin. Daughters - Pernceg Richmond, Malvia Cammerk, Martha Colvin, Elizabeth Rejina, Mary, Susan Ann. Executors - Alfred and William Maberry Harbin; Joseph Drake. Witnesses - Joseph Drake, John McCorkle, James McPherson. Slaves - Clark and Tabby his wife, Harry, Betsey, Peter, Nelson, Dilsy, Louisa, Rachel, Frances, Mahala, Harriet, Melton, Jane, George, Tilda. 31 March 1860. Probated - June 1864, p466.

CHARLES A. PATE

Wife - Mary Ellen Pate. Daughter - Charlin S. E. Pate. Witnesses - F. D. Melton, W. M. Melton, Wm. Carpenter. 27 May 1862. Probated - December 1864, p469.

EDWARD CAGE

Daughters - Martha Elizabeth Matthews, Prisciller Caroline Brewer, Ann Eliza. Executor - Wife, unnamed. Witnesses - Jno. Hicks, J. H. McKay, J. W. S. Merrill. Slaves - Mulinda and her three children, Martha, Sarah, and Mary Francis; Minerva, Harriet and her children, Charlie, Henry, and Ida. 16 December 1864, p470.

LEWIS T. HOWARD

Neice - Olive H. Howard. Nephews - Louis Henry and William R. Moore, sons of Samuel Moore. Brothers - John Q. A. Howard, E. G. Howard dec'd (late of Drew County, Arkansas). Sister - Louisa Moore, dec'd, wife of Samuel Moore. Father - Titus Howard, dec'd. Mentioned - Stephen B. Arnold, Mary L. Moore (daughter of Samuel Moore), Olive I. House Executors - John Q. A. Howard, Saml. Moore, Dr. A. W. Bartlett. Witnesses - R. W. Williamson, M. M. Liddell, Saml. A. Nelson, Wm. L. Hemingway. Slaves - Gricy and her two children, Olive and Louisa; Ben, Phillis. 10 July 1861. Probated - March 1865, p471.

GREENWOOD LEFLORE

Wife - Priscilla Leflore. Son - John D. Leflore. Daughters - Rebecca Harris, Jane. Son-in-law - James C. Harris. Grandsons - Greenwood L. and John B. Halsey, Louis Leflore, Greenwood Leflore, Louis Harris. Mentioned - J. C. Harris, Greenwood Watkins, Daniel Jefferson, Edward Yarbrough. Grandaughters - Martha Davis, Florence Harris. Bequeath to Samuel T. Donley. Owned lands in Carroll, Tallahatchie, Yalobusha & Yazoo Counties, Mississippi and Texas. Executor - Tanner C. Harris. Witnesses - N. H. McCain, Saml. Hart, Wm. A. McCain. Slaves - Amy, Hampton, William, Lizzie, Willis, Hettie. 30 May 1860. Probated - September 1865, 473. (Note: Cemetery marker, Carroll County, Mississippi, Greenwood Leflore b. 3 June 1800 d. 31 August 1865.)

J. H. GOWER

(Nuncupative will.) Wife and children mentioned but not named. Witnesses - G. A. Spivey, A. W. Gary. 4 September 1865. Probated - September 1865, p476.

J. W. McGEHEE

Wife - Emily McGehee. Executor - W. F. Richards. Witnesses - E. T. Baird, J. Irving Scales. 4 March 1862. Probated - September 1865, p477.

ELIJAH M. BECK

Wife - Virginia M. Beck. Executor - Virginia M. Beck. Witnesses - A. M. Nelson, Ira B. Eubanks, Frank D. Price. 14 June 1862. Probated - January 1866, p478.

JOHN HUFFMAN

Wife - Cinthia C. Huffman. Children - Napoleon B., Christopher C., Narcissa D. and William F. Huffman. Executor - Thos. J. Fullilove. Witnesses - E. M. Collins, John Grant, James Yelvingto. 13 December 1862. Probated - 22 March 1866, p479.

ALBERT G. HARVESON

Executor - friend W. Cothran. Witnesses - John A. Fox, W. N. Scales, M. M. Liddell. Slave - Ellen. 21 March 1862. Probated - July 1866, p480.

ALBERT F. McNEILL

Wife - Mary T. McNeill. Children mentioned but not named. Owned property in Choctaw and Attala counties. Executor - W. C. Eskridge. Witnesses - Jane Cohron, A. J. McMeahon, J. J. Andrews. 27 August 1866, p481.

MARTIN A. PURNELL

Wife - Sula C. Purnell. Child - James W. M. Purnell. Brother - M. T. Purnell. Executors - Frank Hawkins, Sula C. Purnell. Witnesses - W. H. Hairston, F. C. Oldham, A. I. Sanderson. 9 August 1864 (at Camp Vaiden Artillery). Probated - Nov. 1866, p483. (Note: Coleman Cemetery, Carroll County, Mississippi, Martin A. Purnell b. 1 Dec. 1842 d. 23 Sept. 1866.

MRS. MARGARET H. SANDERS

Neices & nephews - Almira Ann Crose and her three brothers Wetey G. Davis, Fielding Davis and John Halsy Davis; Mary Louisa Peets. Brother - Richard Davis. Executor - Richard Davis. Witnesses - I. S. Johnson, B. B. Love, Falba Johnson. Bequeaths to - Martha D. A. Griffin, Mary Eliza Peets, George Halsey Peets, Wiley G. Davis, Almira Ambrose. Slaves - Malvina, Ivy, Charles and his wife Mary. 8 February 1858. Protated - November 1865, p485.

A. B. BULLARD

Wife - Martha Susan Bullard. Two youngest children - James Paul and William Arthur. Son - Clarance Bullard. Daughters - Laura Rachel, Mary Elizabeth, Betty, and Emma Dale Bullard. Brother - Elijah G. Bullard. Brother-in-law - Lemuel/Samuel J. Copeland. Bequeath to friend William G. Thomas. Executor - A. M. Nelson. Witnesses - A. M. Nelson, Saml. Hart, B. R. Mayes. 11 December 1866, p489.

CHARLES JONES

Brothers - Gil Jones and Jacob H. Jones. Mentioned - Mrs. Henrietta Heggie, Mrs. M. R. Heggie. Witnesses - James S. Heggie. 22 January 1867, p493.

SARAH PARHAM (alias Turner)

Grandchildren - (children of Dr. Samuel W. Vaughn), (children of David B. Turner). Granddaughter - Susan Alice Vaughn. Grandsons - Dr. David B. Turner, William Turner, Henry W. Vaughn. Stepson - Simon T. Turner (his wife - Martha A. Turner). Daughters of Simon T. Turner - Martha A. E. Turner, Sally Margaret. Stepson - John T. Turner. Daughters of John T. Turner - Mary, Martha, Virginia Lucy, Evelin, Sally. Executor - Dr. David B. Turner. Witnesses - Jesse Holman, Simon T. Turner. Slaves - Anderson, Sidney, Nancy, Easter, Emiline, Ann, Henry, William, Woodson, Eliza, Sally, Frank, Mary. 21 January 1862. Probated - December 1866, p494.

JAMES McCAULLA/McCARLY

Sons - William, John, James. Daughters - Nancy Holland, Mary E. Williams, Jenny Davis, Emma Morris, Martha B. Corbin, Caroline Davidson, Amanda Ann McCaulla (youngest). Wife - mentioned but not named. Executor - Peter McCaskill. Witnesses - O. L. Kimbrough, H. H. Hudgins, R. Nelson. 8 March 1865, p496.

ALEXANDER GRAY

Wife - Martha P. Gray. Daughter - Martha Susan Stancill, dec'd. Sons - James H. Gray, dec'd (his wife was Mary E. Gray), William P. Gray, dec'd. Grandchildren - Alexander Stancill (son of Martha S. Stancill), Alice C. Gray (only child of James H. Gray), William Gray (only child of William P. Gray by his last wife Emily Gray). Executor - Martha P. Gray. Witnesses - O. L. Kimbrough, Wm. Billups, James O. Bradley. 8 August 1862. Probated - 1867, p498.

JAMES O'NEAL

Wife - Ann O'Neal. Witnesses - J. K. Allen, John W. Dunn. 28 July 1867. Probated - September 1867, p501.

EDITH BLANKS

Daughter - Mary Bartlett. Executor - A. W. Bartlett. Witnesses - J. C. Gray, J. T. Redfern. 15 April 1861. Probated - October 1867, p502.

SARAH H. BILLINGSLEY

Sons - W. C. Billingsley, Thomas W. Billingsley, dec'd. Children - J. E. Holman, A. E. Trotter. Executor - W. C. Billingsley. Witnesses - J. W. Holman, C. G. Holman, S. Applegate. January 1867. Probated - February 1867, p505.

J. W. SANDERS

Wife - Mary J. Sanders. Son - Benjamin Sanders. Disobedient Daughter - Martha J. Sturdivan. Mentioned - O. J. Moore. Witnesses - J. A. Campbell, T. Trotter, Jacob M. Bachman. 14 January 1868. Probated - March 1868, p507.

MARY J. STOKES

Requested she be buried at Spring Hill Church cemetery beside late son William P. Stokes. Bequeaths to - William N. Penn (of State of Missouri), Paul Penn (of Grenada, Mississippi), C. E. Penn, Sequs M. Kyle's children, Annie Wallace, daughter of James Penn, Parnelia Kile's children, Elizabeth Day's children, C. E. Penn, Creed Penn. Mentioned - Jack Johnson. Witnesses - J. R. Fielden, H. M. Bristol, N. C. Koon. Negroes - Ailcy & Lilly. 24 March 1868. Probated - July 1868, p508.

DAVID W. ANDERSON

Wife - Sarah H. Anderson. Daughters - Nancy Baskins, Mary Anderson, Unis America McClerge. Bequeaths to - Levi Anderson, George Anderson, David Anderson, Gains Anderson, Roxanna Bagley, Martha Brown. Executor - Dr. A. J. Sanderson. Witnesses - W. A. Cagle, A. J. Anderson, B. J. Causey. 29 December 1866. Probated - June 1868, p510.

JAMES WELLONS

Wife - Cynthia Wellons. Sons - Benjamin H. Wellons and George P. Wellons. Daughters mentioned but not named. Executors - Benjamin H. & George P. Wellons. Witnesses - J. C. McCaldwell, Wm. L, Hemingway, R. W. Williamson. 21 July 1868. Probated - September 1868, p512.

STEPHEN B. ARNOLD

Wife - Elizure Arnold. Father - Levi Arnold, dec'd. Neices & nephews - John W., James A. & Roger Q. Shackelford; and

George W., Durant L., Stephen Arnold, Mary Grider, Julia F. Lock, and heirs of Levi W. Arnold of Texas. Mentioned - William E. Duke. Executor - Elizure Arnold. Witnesses - G. A. Graves, J. R. Shackelford, Creed Penn. 15 August 1868, p514.

ROBERT KIRKWOOD

Brother - William and his wife Rachel. Neice - Narcissa Hudson, wife of Alfred Hudson. Executor - William Kirkwood. Witnesses - W. Cothran, W. B. Helm, Chas. Kopperl. 13 June 1856. Probated - September 1868, p517. (Note: will of William Kirkwood, Carroll County Will Bk. A, p146.)

JOSEPH J. DAVIS

Wife - Emily M. Davis. Children - Joseph L., Mary C. Willard H., Balfour S., Fannie E., Leonida L. Davis. Executor - Emily M. Davis. Witnesses - A. W. Montgomery, S. G. Lane, John R. Applewhite. 3 July 1869. Probated - August 1869.

RAN. TISDALE

Daughter - Jacky Ann Smith. Mentioned - L. Jake Baskins. Executor - Dr. William Ward. Witnesses - Frank Hawkins, J. A. H. Haslett, A. W. Bismuke. 6 April 1867. Probated - September 1869, p520.

MARY J. HUDSON

Child - Marion Hudson. Mentioned - Wallace & Alfred Somerville, sons of James Somerville. Executor - friend John Cain. Witnesses - J. Z. George, J. C. Anderson, Wm. Mattox. 20 October 1869. Probated - 15 Nov. 1869, p522.

TRIPHENA MONEY

Husband - Pearson Money. Daughter - Mary E. Love. Children mentioned but not named. Grandchildren - Richard C. Fox, John Somerfield Fox. Executor - Pearson Money. Witnesses - Wm. Ewing, S. W. Boyan, H. S. Sanders. 5 January 1870. Probated - February 1870, p523.

JOHN DUNCAN

(Of Jackson, Mississippi.) Family - Walker, my first born; Lucy, the young the bright and intellectual; the beloved wife of my bosom; Mary, my peerless daughter; and Garnet, the last and youngest. Neice - Mary Jane Duncan (alias Mary McFarland Duncan) daughter of deceased brother William Duncan. Sisters - Mary, the widow of Charles Stewart; Louisa

Brodie, wife of George Payn Quackenboss, Jane A. Duncan, unmarried (residing in New York). Nephew - L. Alex Duncan, brother of Mary J. Duncan. Brother-in-law - George P. Quackenboss (of New York City). Witnesses - Fred J. Stanton (of Washington, D. C.) & Duncan S. Walker (of Washington, D. C.) 11 December 1865. Probated - February 1872, p525.

MARGARET J. McCAMPBELL

Neices - Sarah Emily Moore, wife of James E. Moore, Mary Flora Nelson, Emily E. Moore Nephews - Frank Crawford Nelson, James H. Nelson, Andrew M. Nelson. Sister - Eliza Nelson. Brother - Andrew McCampbell (of Knox County, Tennessee). Neice-in-law - Mary Ann Nelson, wife of Wm. E. Nelson; Mary F. Nelson, wife of James H. Nelson; Laura F. Nelson, wife of Andrew M. Nelson. Great-neice - Mary A. Clements. Great-nephew - Charles C. Clements. Mentioned - Dr. E. R. McLean. Witnesses - Benjn. Roach, Benjn. F. Roach. 3 September 1869. Probated - December 1873, p529.

HENRY S. FARMER

Wife - Margaret A. Farmer. Children mentioned but not named. Witnesses - Jas. E. Farmer, E. M. Whitehead, J. E. Summer. July 1873. Probated - 6 April 1875, p533.

J. A. H. HASLETT

Wife - Mary E. Haslett. Nephews - John A. and Wm. W. McBride. Bequeath to friend H. J. McBride. Executor - Mary E. Haslett. Witnesses - Frank Hawkins, P. H. Cain, W. W. Conger. March 1872. p534.

REV. JAMES APPLEWHITE

Wife - Mary Ann Applewhite. Heirs - John, William, Joseph and Ralph Applewhite. Mentioned - Rev. William Holmes. Witnesses - F. H. Grantham, Ross Calhoun. 20 July 1871, p536.

R. W. W. LIDDELL

Wife - Elizabeth Ann Liddell. Son - James M. Liddell. Children mentioned but not named. Executors - Elizabeth Ann and James M. Liddell. Witnesses - J. O. Sanders, G. F. Neill. Jr., H. J. Liddell. 5 July 1875. Probated - July 1875, p537.

COL. WM. BOOTH

Son - Thomas Booth. Mentioned - T. H. & J. M. Allen of

New Orleans, W. P. West, John J. Hooker, firm of Booth & West, John C. McKenzie, Mrs. Sallie Cline, Mrs. Julia Roberts, H. H. Booth. Executor - Thomas Booth. Witnesses - J. D. Brantley, John Erskin, J. J. Carnes. 12 April 1875, p539.

JAMES E. LOTT

Wife - Sarah E. Lott. Executor - Sarah E. Lott. Witnesses - Thos. W. Sullivan, W. R. Mullen. Probated - September 1875, p542.

INDEX